LET US WAKE

A Quantum Journey to Spiritual Awakening, Higher Consciousness, and Inner Peace

van deburg

Contents

Foreword

My intent is to provide information that will help you see beyond the illusion of reality we experience in our daily lives, bridge the gap to understanding the beauty and purpose of our world, and put you on the right path to take control of your health and well-being.

This information is straight-forward and easy to comprehend, but the majority will likely find difficulty in acceptance. Only those that keep an open mind, set aside all preconceived ideas and overcome any psychological defense mechanisms will have the choice to break free from the control systems that prevent us from discovering our true nature.

Most of us believe that we are too busy to investigate or consider ourselves previously well-informed, even when the issues are of great importance and our instincts warn us that what we are being told is untrue. That, like much that manifests in our world, is by intelligent and deceptive design. Absolutely nothing we experience happens by accident and there is no such thing as coincidence. Every event we accept as such further removes us from reality, until we become so far removed that the simple truth seems absurd and we often dismiss the very things that could easily improve or transform our lives.

"The ultimate ignorance is the rejection of something you know nothing about and refuse to investigate" - Dr. Wayne Dyer. I was often discouraged by the consistency of the responses when I recommended proven effective solutions that would enable people to overcome their issues: "I don't believe in that", "If that were true, everybody would be doing it" and "I don't have the time", until I realized what they were really telling me was; if there is a better way, I refuse to even consider it.

Many of us have become totally dependent on qualified professionals to determine what is best for us because we believe that we have no choice. Some refuse to explore less popular methods because they have been misled by the media or some other trusted source, or they appear too good to be true. "The pressure to fit in with one's social peers can be irresistible. To a human lemming, the logic behind an opinion doesn't count as much as the power and popularity behind an opinion" - Norman Livergood.

The more we are subjected to what is false, the more difficult it becomes to determine what is true. We should begin by questioning our current beliefs and ridding any delusions in order to realize the existing possibilities where we experience wellness, love and compassion without judgment and fear. We should end with the understanding that you have abilities far greater than you can currently imagine, and only you will be capable of determining what is best for you once they are realized.

gnothe seauton

Chapter One

Free Your Mind

Three ships were anchored off the coast of North America in the late fifteenth century. The Native Americans had not encountered ships and had no knowledge that such things exist. For that reason, they were initially unable to see them. One of the elders noticed that the water was being affected, and the unusual patterns kept his focus on the area of the ships. He concentrated for a long time, until he was able to see them slowly appear.

The other natives there were able to see the ships after the elder described them and they concentrated on the same area. Eventually all natives were able to see ships when they first encountered them because they had the innate knowledge that such things exist.

There is much happening around us that goes unnoticed. All our senses are based on association and comparison. They are nothing more than electrical signals transmitted to the brain, where they are compared to existing information to achieve sensations and predict outcomes. Do you see, hear, smell, taste, and feel in your dreams? Of course, so how do you know you are not in a dream right now, a seemingly long one? What if you discovered that you are co-controlling this dream and have the ability to help change it?

Much more on that later, now I should explain that most of the findings I will address herein have been scientifically or clinically proven and documented. I have tested them with numerous sources or personal experience and found them to be true; however, please do not believe anything without testing it for yourself and finding it to be true.

Please investigate anything unfamiliar and make your own discoveries. A world of possibilities will emerge, and you will begin to see things for what they are. Keep in mind that you will often encounter conflicting information. I ask that you view it, along with any related information you have to this point, with the same scientific objectivity, regardless of the source.

You might begin to regain your instinctive and guiding curiosity. You might choose to receive the information you have been overlooking and the innate knowledge you have been ignoring. You might keep asking yourself, "why?", until you acquire the external information you need to find the answers within yourself. You might find that self-education leads to self-knowledge, self-awareness and self-reliance, and you might discover that inspiration and intuition take us very far when properly utilized.

You might think there is no time for any of that, but I believe that once you start feeding your mind the good stuff, you will find it suits you. You might even begin to lose interest in network television, sports, and other things we often think we can't live without that consume countless hours of our time.

You would be amazed at the time you have when the television is off and think of the time currently spent dealing with problems you could soon have the knowledge to solve by simply considering new information. We often make the mistake of believing that some issues are too big to address; however, something done once daily or weekly, like reading something new and informative, switching a food or beverage, trying a new exercise, or learning how to meditate and focus, really adds up over months and years.

We all remember this encouraging phrase, "You will never know unless you try". That just doesn't seem to entice us anymore. In fact, a multitude of logical statements somehow lose their value over time. Sure, we get busy and preoccupied. There are always issues that demand immediate attention and goals that require long-term focus; but why do we really lose the desire to learn? What leads us to believe that no significant scientific and spiritual discoveries are taking place today, and if there are, why do they seem unworthy of our time and attention? Why have we not heard of them before?

Homeostasis

The best path to any solution is to determine the source of the problem, the cause behind the effect. One cause behind our reluctance to consider new information is known as *homeostasis*, which is *the mind and body's resistance to change*. There is necessary homeostasis, such as body temperature, heart rate and sleep cycle regulation; however, there is also limiting homeostasis, such as resistance to changes in our diets, habits, scientific understandings, and spiritual beliefs. There is an underlying dynamic tension between homeostasis and necessary change, and we often remain in our comfort zones to keep our lives consistent and predictable, which limits the possibility for growth and inhibits our ability to adapt.

Our bodies and minds are constantly changing, and we can begin to see all the available solutions and possibilities if we can release our attachment to permanence. First we must understand that we are contending with the balance between homeostasis and creative change, and that both are crucial to our well-being. Then we must begin to pay close attention and not judge, label or dismiss information and people we are "drawn to". You will soon realize that everything we experience is telling us something about ourselves, and it is critical that we listen and understand. In many cases, simply becoming and staying aware is all that is necessary. Just remember to ask yourself questions like, "Why did I have that reaction to what I just read and what if it were true, why am I feeling this way and what am I experiencing in this moment?" That's how we begin to see our true self and surroundings.

The Media

The other cause behind the effect is the disinformation we receive from the media, both mainstream and alternative sources. I am not going to explain how the media works to get you upset or involved, we are going to address it so you will wishfully choose to no longer be upset or involved. We can put it behind us and move forward once we see it for what it is. Some of the things you will discover here might be initially painful. We all like to think that we have a solid handle on reality, and no one likes discovering that they have been misled. Many of us have been conditioned by the media to reject information that makes us uncomfortable. "A truth's initial commotion is directly proportional to how deeply the lie was believed. It wasn't the world being round that agitated people, but that the world wasn't flat. When a well-packaged web of lies has been sold gradually to the masses over generations, the truth will seem utterly preposterous and its speaker a raving lunatic" - Dresden James. "All truth passes through three stages. First it is ridiculed, second it is violently opposed, and third it is accepted as self-evident" - Arthur Schopenhauer. "The truth will set you free, but not until it is finished with you" - David Foster Wallace. Please remain objective, stay in the question, and you will be set free.

About ninety percent of us get our news from corporate network sources. Most of those polled state they do not believe what they see and hear on the news but ask them for their opinion on a certain topic and you will get the exact same information they just told you they do not believe. Furthermore, ask someone that does not watch network news and programming for their opinion on that same topic, and you will most likely get the same information. That is due to the intrusive general consensus created by mainstream media. It is almost impossible to escape. It's in our workplaces, newsstands, bookstores, internet sites, restaurants, bars, airports, cars, homes, subconscious, and history books. Yes, the stories in the media today will be in our history books tomorrow and that has been going on for a very long time. It is just as Mary Croft stated when she came to this realization about her third-grade teacher, "She could tell us *anything*."

That is alarmingly true because even a wise and well-informed teacher can be conditioned to believe what she is teaching or forced to teach what she does not believe. It seems the goal in education today is to remove the teachers, who are viewed as potential sources of reason and common sense, from the classrooms and replace them with monitors. Teachers are often the children's last line of defense. Without them, the information goes directly to the student and there is little opportunity for anyone to question it, which is exactly what everyone should be doing; questioning everything we are told.

We are conditioned from birth to never question authority, and children are ridiculed for it in the classroom. Many bright minds are stifled, diagnosed and medicated to keep them from questioning what their instincts are telling them is wrong. That obviously needs to stop, and we must stop settling for opinions formed by others that we can believe in without any thought and effort. We must stop believing that we can find the truth if we remain submerged in this sea of disinformation long enough. It is all basically the same misleading information. It is all propaganda.

Manufacture Of Consent

What comes to mind when you hear someone say, "propaganda"? Maybe Nazi fliers dropped from planes, or some made-up story designed to make you think a certain way. Actually, both are correct, except today we have a much more sophisticated delivery system than fliers dropped from planes.

First let's go back even further to when highly organized state propaganda was used during the first world war. The word, *propaganda*, did not have any negative connotations until it was associated with Nazi Germany after the second world war. It simply meant *information*. The British had a Ministry of Information that they used to lure the United States into the first world war, by fabricating Hun stories and other tall tales, because they were definitely going to lose otherwise. The MOI mainly targeted American intellectuals on the assumption that they were the ones most likely to believe the propaganda and disseminate it through their system. The supporting British Ministry of Information documents have been released and state that their ultimate goal was to control the thought of the civilized world.

Obviously, it worked. In the United States, Woodrow Wilson was elected on an anti-war platform with the slogan, "Peace without victory". It was a pacifist country and very opposed to war, especially on foreign soil. Propaganda was the only way to turn the population into raving anti-Germans, so they created the first U.S. propaganda agency called the Creel Commission, also known as the Committee of Public Information, which created an aggressive hysteria, and the country was able to enter the war.

Adolf Hitler was very impressed with the achievements of the British Ministry of Information and the Creel Commission. He stated in Mein Kampf that Germany lost the first world war because they were overwhelmed by British and American propaganda. He developed his own propaganda system for the second world war, which included the "terrorist" bombing of their parliament building.

After the war the Creel Commission applied their experience and turned their attention to the problem of the United States becoming more formally democratic. New immigrants were constantly arriving, and too many problematic people could vote and participate. It was getting difficult for the elite to run things as planned, so they utilized the ones who had perfected the art of controlling what people think.

The leading figure in the Creel Commission was Edward Bernays, who was made famous by the campaigns he ran in the late 1920s, which convinced many women to smoke, and his public relations effort behind the U.S.-backed coup that overthrew the democratic government of Guatemala. He wrote a book titled Propaganda in the year 1928, which explained that it is possible to regiment the public mind every bit as much as an army regiments their bodies, and the techniques of regimentation must be used by the intelligent minorities to make sure the majority stays on the right course.

Another member of the Creel Commission was Walter Lippmann, a powerful man in journalism, who wrote essays on false democracy and the application of propaganda. His book titled Public Opinion introduced a new method of control that he called Manufacture of Consent. "By manufacturing consent, we can overcome the fact that formally a lot of people have the right to vote. We can make it irrelevant because we can make sure that their choices and attitudes will be structured in such a way that they will always do what we tell them, even if they have a formal way to participate."

Harold Glasswell, the founder of Communications and Academic Political Science, openly published his studies of propaganda, which clearly outline the same agenda. Now all this information is within mainstream literature, but it's only for the people on the inside. It is not openly discussed or taught at any school or university. Just like we will never be taught what James Madison stated during the constitutional convention; that the main goal of the new system must be to protect the minority of the opulent against the majority and must be designed so that it achieves that end. That is the basis of the constitutional system, but it is not studied and most are unaware because it is well-hidden in the academic scholarship.

Over the years the art of manufacturing consent has evolved into an exact science, utilized by major corporations and the government, which have become one in the same and are assisted by the bankers, who are controlled by and indebted to the Federal Reserve, a private bank that prints private notes. A common method is Problem-Reaction-Solution. For example, a tragedy, such as a bombing or shooting, occurs and is exploited in the media to achieve a specific reaction from the public. The reaction is always fear and disgust with a demand for protection and assistance, and the solution always requires a reduction of your liberties and an increase in your dependence.

A recurring practice of manufacture of consent is the presidential election. The media coverage begins about eighteen months before the elections and dominates many people's thoughts. We are led to believe that we can make a difference by voting and there is little else we can do. We are split into two groups, democrats and republicans, for one purpose; divide and conquer. The party that gets elected ultimately blames the other for not being able to fulfill their obligations, and we fight among ourselves.

We should see by now that it does not matter who reads from the teleprompter. The same policies and procedures are going to be implemented because they were planned many years before. The Bush/Gore election fiasco eliminated the manual tabulation process and inferred legitimacy, but it has always been a charade to occupy our thoughts and make us believe that we are participating. It is all based on a false premise, and once a false premise is established, then everything within it is false. It does not matter how much it is analyzed and explained, or how many charts and graphs are produced. It is all untrue.

The Mass Media

All this deception through the use of propaganda is only made possible by the media, and there are different types which do different things. First we have the entertainment media, or mass media, which diverts and directs the mass audience. They realize that we will make little time to think for ourselves and concentrate on important matters if we are obsessed with drama, celebrities, sex scandals, and sports. So, let's take a look at the most effective delivery system for mass media propaganda, the television:

Television, in and of itself, is not a *bad* thing, only how it is used could be viewed as good or bad. More than seventy-five percent of all commercial television time is paid for by the one hundred largest corporations and some of them spend billions of dollars per year. They force the producers to edit and make specific additions to their scripts, making most commercial television a private medium for their use only.

Modern televisions emit theta waves, and the flicker rate (the time between frames) is at the optimum speed to cause the brain to vibrate at alpha level. When we watch, we are placed in a hypnotic state of consciousness, where we are most receptive to information at the subconscious level, then the images and suggestions are implanted directly into the mind without viewer participation. Television violence stimulates our fight or flight instinct, and we are forced to suppress it since we cannot act upon it, creating a cycle of impulse and suppression that causes confusion and leaves an emotional charge. After watching, some of the adrenaline is released through frantic behavior or childhood hyperactivity and the rest accumulates in the body.

When we watch reality and talk shows, dramas and sitcoms, we subconsciously identify with one or more of the characters and their beliefs and actions are incorporated into our own. In the *real* world, we do not consciously ponder what they would do in a particular scenario, it all happens without any conscious awareness. The subconscious mind automatically compares circumstances from countless characters, which influences our decisions and even forms our opinions.

We are always receiving and retaining information at the subconscious level, even during sleep. That is where most of our ideas and views about our world originate, and why our thoughts are not our own if we subject ourselves to television programming. That's why they call it "programming".

Small children and infants most definitely understand and retain all the information they receive at the subconscious level. Sleeping with the television on prevents REM sleep, as well as any conscious resistance to the suggestive information being received. Have you ever watched a program or film and found yourself unable to "snap out of it" or sat through something you did not even want to watch? It can take up to forty-five minutes to get out of the hypnotic state of consciousness after the show is over.

We also experience time compression and time expansion during programming. An example of time compression is when all the boring stuff we normally experience is omitted. We do not have to watch the characters go to the bathroom, ride the subway or get stuck in traffic for an hour. They go from scene to scene with no down time. A story that might take years to unfold can be compressed into an hour of climaxes. That makes our daily lives seem dull by comparison and is one of the reasons we are always in a hurry. Have you ever had plenty of time to drive somewhere, but still felt stressed out and impatient with the other drivers? Do you often find yourself wishing time away to be elsewhere?

Time expansion is when the good moments are slowed down or repeated to be viewed and enjoyed much longer than we could normally experience them. Without slow motion, pause and rewind, we feel like we're missing something, or cling to a good moment because it will be over much too soon.

Before detected and banned, subliminal messages were projected every fifth frame of some films to subconsciously influence the viewers' desires. Modern picture resolution is totally captivating and almost everyone can experience it since the digital upgrades. Of course, the actual content of the programming becomes slightly more intrusive, misleading and damaging every day. Please consider what content and behavior is now deemed harmless and even appropriate, as compared to ten years ago, then twenty or more if you are old enough. If you were around in the 1980s, you might remember that there were few commercials on cable (pay) television when it was introduced. We have become like the frog that did not jump out of the boiling pot because the temperature was turned up slowly.

And then there are the advertisements. We all realize that the intent is to sell us something, often something we do not want or need, but many do not realize how powerful they are. The components of most commercial advertisements are based on psychological experimentation and previous success. The repetition, word selection, voice pitch and tone, symbols, sights, and sounds affect us at the subconscious level and influence much more than just our desire for the product.

If we look at what is being advertised, we see that insurance, electronic devices and plans, automobiles, beer, and fast food each account for approximately ten percent of all commercials, and about ten percent are for miscellaneous products and services. That leaves a huge percentage and helps pave the way for just one industry.

Forty percent of all commercial advertisements are for prescription and over-the-counter drugs. It seems that everyone uses them, they are safe, easy to obtain, and even recommended. That is why most of us believe that we need them and ignore the sources behind the symptoms. I will explain why we often do not need them in the chapter of empowerment, for now let's look at one of the tactics used by the drug industry:

Ever wonder why the side effects are advertised more than the claimed benefits? Why not just disclose them in the fine print or explain them when the medication is prescribed? They do it because they want you to accept the side effects immediately, then go to the doctor with the intent of obtaining the advertised drug. Let's say there are four advertised side effects for a particular drug, like loss of vision, headaches, upset stomach, and vertigo. The patient takes the medication, experiences the first two, and gets some initial symptom relief. They are more likely to endure the side effects and take the drug if they believe it's not comparatively harmful and it could be a lot worse.

Fast food and beer are extremely well-advertised sources of illness and obesity, and perfect examples of the illusion supported by the media. The vibrant and healthy people joyfully serving and consuming them without a care are rarely what we find at the fast-food restaurants and sports bars.

The Elite Media

The next type of media is the elite media, the ones with huge resources, such as the New York Times, NBC and CBS. They set the agendas and framework in which the rest of the media operates. Every day the Associated Press sends a notice to television and news editors explaining what stories are news and what they are supposed to report. An editor really has no options because they do not have the resources to discover what is news, and if they report stories the elite media does not approve of, they will not be an editor much longer. All elite media corporations are owned by or directly linked to the world's largest corporations. They are at the very top of the private economy power structure, which is completely tyrannical. All major corporations, including the media, are unquestionably hierarchic and you either accept and internalize their methods or find another career.

The elite media is a doctrinal system, and they interact closely with other major corporations, the government and the universities. For example, a reporter writing a big story will go to a well-known university or foundation and find an expert that will inform them what to write. Universities are not independent institutions and are dependent on outside sources of support, such as private wealth, major corporations and the government. The people within them that cannot accept, believe and internalize what they are told are weeded out, and there are many filtering devices and ways to get rid of people that think independently.

Most people that have experienced college know that the educational system is highly geared toward rewarding conformity and obedience. The elite, upscale institutions, such as Princeton, Harvard and Oxford, are focused on socialization and concentrate on manners, upper class behavior and how to think the right thoughts. When you go through the elite education system, you learn that there are some things you are not allowed to say and certain thoughts you are not allowed to have.

Even if you were to study academic political science or journalism, you would not likely encounter any information that exposes the truth about how corporations and governments fabricate the news. Why would the elite entities that support the universities allow any critical analysis of what they are doing? They wouldn't and they don't. That is how many intelligent, highly educated people have no idea what's really going on and why the bad actors, with great hair and make-up, reading stories from teleprompters are just as clueless as the poor souls that watch them. They typically believe in what they are reporting because they would not have made it to their positions without internal acceptance.

Does that mean that all network news is untrue? No, effective propaganda is ninety percent truth and ten percent is the con. You will occasionally get the complete truth if it somehow benefits the ones reporting. I am referring to the handful of entities that control all network media outlets. For example, the same corporation that owned the Wall Street Journal during the economic crisis in the year 2008 also owned the largest newspaper in the world and the Fox Network, so who's guarding the hen house?

The Alternative Media

About ten percent of the population get their news from alternative sources. I view many of them as clever traps to catch those that learn the truth about mainstream media and direct their energy to predetermined issues. That was confirmed when I discovered how most of them are funded. Some non-profit sources are funded by the same or similar entities that own the elite media, and others often reflect the views of their advertisers or include links to sites that contradict their stories. Conflicting information from a single source often creates confusion and doubt in the recipient and they will most likely believe what they have heard before, the mainstream view.

You might have heard the statement, "We will lead every revolution against ourselves". It's a very effective tactic utilized by elite power structures. The media provides enough truth about a certain topic to occupy your mind, get you involved and drain your energy. A common method of manufacturing and controlling dissent is selectively instructing or permitting politicians and podcasters to blow the whistle on predetermined conspiracies and government cover-ups in an effort to distract us and divert our attention.

We are directly or indirectly encouraged to sign petitions, attend critical meetings and participate in organized protests. That keeps us focused on the predetermined issues and prevents us from uncovering what they do not want us to know. It's called Group Think, a method to control, manipulate and keep track of those that oppose the corporate agenda. This idea will make more sense soon, but when you "fight" against a cause, you give it your energy, which strengthens the very thing you oppose. You are externally battling something placed before you to internally conquer. “Be the change you want to see” - Gandhi, was not intended to encourage organized protesting. He was referring to the process of being an example of the change and believing in the desired outcome as reality in order to help it manifest.

I found that many stories reported by the alternative media eventually make it to the networks, who put their spin on things and lead us to believe that what they are reporting is as deep as it goes. That causes viewers to think they have been well-informed and have no need to explore any further.

We believe we discover who are behind our problems through the alternative media, which causes us to experience resentment, hate and other forms of fear, which creates an emotional charge that leads to stress and other issues. It makes it difficult to understand that there really are no *evil* people, and we are all here to do what we're all here to do. It seems as if there is only bad news when we view the world through the corporate news media, which removes us from the truth that there is beauty and purpose in everything.

If you feel you must know what is taking place around the world, it would be wise to do your own research and draw logical conclusions, as opposed to effortlessly relying on the media to inform you. “History is a fable agreed upon” - Napoleon Bonaparte. “If you are not careful, the newspapers will have you hating the oppressed and loving the oppressors” - Malcolm X.

Knowledge Is Power

I trust that was sufficient information for you to understand how the media works and how it all came about. Many truths become evident as we realize that knowledge is power, so let's explore how simple it is for those in power to keep beneficial information and empowering truths out of sight and mind:

One method is falsely adding something which makes the original story unbelievable. Another is excluding important facts and supporting information that would validate the original story. Pictures and videos are very powerful, and misleading explanations are often provided. They also write scripts and run stories that acknowledge, then tactfully dismiss any information that could expose the truth and hurt their profits. An example is reporting something that is gaining in popularity, such as nutritional healing or meditation, to appear objective, then omitting the critical supporting facts to make it appear insignificant. Natural, proven effective methods can be made to appear as New Age theories or fads.

The easiest way to keep the truth and empowering information from us is simply to not report it. We are programmed to believe that we're getting the only news worthy of our attention, and anything not reported must be a conspiracy theory or superstition. And we should be more careful with statements like, "That's only make-believe, it's not real", which can be comforting to someone frightened by what they have seen but can also lead us to believe that many beneficial actualities are impossibilities.

All types of media work together to support the illusion. We have our "trusted" news sources and our "harmless" shows and commercials to tell us what's going on and how we are supposed to behave, and all elite media company owners (there are only five now, all others are subsidiaries) are indirectly working together. They may be competing against each other but share a much larger common goal.

We can conclude that the media are owned by wealthy and powerful people, who control what topics reach the public. What is reported and not reported serves the united agenda of the mega corporations, the government and the enforcing systems that support them. The general population is viewed as ignorant and meddlesome outsiders, who are terrible judges of their own best interests. We are to be workers, consumers and spectators- not participants. We are provided with the illusion of choice in order to keep us unaware of their motives and dependent on their protection, advice and products. They should simply be seen for what they are and not allowed to invoke any form of fear within us.

Breaking Free

Do you remember your initial experience with a computer? You probably needed frequent assistance or training and only became proficient after you knew how to work the equipment. Now think of your mind as a computer with the ability to reason but operating at a fraction of its potential power.

Most of us never get the assistance and training we need to learn how to use our equipment; however, there are those that do know how to use it and they are very proficient. They utilize the correct words, sights, sounds, shapes, symbols, colors, chemicals, fragrances, and frequencies required to trigger specific reactions. We can learn how to use our equipment, reclaim our thoughts and operate at a higher power if we stop downloading bad information, start downloading good information, become aware of our true surroundings, and pay close attention to everything we experience.

How do we stop downloading bad information? We can begin by separating ourselves from the corporate media as much as possible, which gives us an instant increase in time and mental clarity, and an instant decrease in stress and irritability. The media are a powerful form of addiction that should not be taken lightly; fortunately, there are two effective ways to conquer addiction:

One is the three-week method. We can overcome most addictions if we separate ourselves from the source for twenty-one days. I stopped watching network television and lost the desire to watch it after approximately three weeks. Later I decided to watch the season opener of a science-fiction drama I once enjoyed but was appalled by something I could not identify, becoming irritated for no apparent reason, until I finally realized what was happening.

We all know we get a junk body if we feed it junk food. We also get a junk mind if we feed it junk information, and I was experiencing my mind's resistance to the garbage I was consuming again. It's very similar to someone introducing a toxin, such as alcohol or MSG, and the body rejecting it. The reaction is not as strong the next time and eventually the body just struggles to repair the continuing damage. The three-week detoxification period had allowed my mind and instincts to reset, and the irritability was a symptom caused by reintroducing the deceptive and destructive information.

The other way is the slow, steady and sure method, in which we gradually withdraw and stick to the plan until the desire is gone. That can take longer but is often more feasible and less difficult than going "cold turkey". It's always beneficial to set goals and time frames, depending on the situation; although, too many rules and regulations might be a set-up for failure and frustration. It's important not to tell ourselves that we will never watch network television again, or whatever the addiction may be, that tends to make it taboo, and some things are okay in moderation. The key is to become more aware of the consequences and realize that the habit is the real problem.

Both methods are extremely effective when we substitute something healthy, beneficial and satisfying for the addictive item. There are many wonderful substitutions for the media, they are just less obvious and will not be selected and presented in the same fashion. We can also utilize both methods and decide which one to use for a particular addiction. For example, I used the three-week method for network television and the slow, steady and sure method for fast and processed foods, and I had no idea how unhealthy they were until I was free from them. They are the "unknown" causes of many mental and physical health issues. Obviously, it's easier to stay clean once the source and habit are out of our systems, especially when reintroducing them makes us sick and the right substitutions make us well.

Moving Forward

How do we start downloading *good* information? What are the *right* substitutions for the media? What *truth* is being kept from us? See... you are already asking the right questions. We find that the veil is lifted and the smoke clears once we are no longer concentrating on false-premise systems. Our instincts and common sense take over and the connection to our innate knowledge is realized and continuously strengthened. Two objects cannot occupy the same space, and our minds become like vacuums as we take out the garbage and get rid of the clutter.

You will probably find yourself wondering why you did not come to know so many simple and beautiful things sooner. I recently read some very enlightening books that were written long before I was born. I thought I had really been missing something all these years but then realized that they would not have been beneficial to me before I discovered them because I was not ready for the information. I would have dismissed it and possibly never considered it again. It is no coincidence that you are reading this book. Again, there is no such thing as coincidence. This found its way to you because you are ready for it now. Your existing knowledge has been serving a purpose, and it is your time to have new understandings so they can serve a purpose.

It is wise to be aware of the difference between beliefs and understandings. There are some things we must believe in without any doubt, such as our ability to heal and manifest; however, we often close our minds to existing possibilities when we form beliefs and firm opinions about what is best for us and others. We should view our knowledge as temporary understandings that must be continuously tested against new information in order to stay in the question, the best place from which to learn.

We should be careful not to dismiss an entire body or source of new information because we disagree with one part or aspect. The part we do not believe could have been added for that reason, but it could be that we are just unfamiliar or experiencing homeostasis. Let's say we research the part we do not believe and come to the understanding that it is simply not true. That does not mean that everything we learned from that source is false. The key is to gather information from numerous sources and trust your instincts, your gut feelings- not the popular opinion, and the best information becomes evident.

Information is not knowledge. Knowledge is knowing. It is only attained by finding the answers within yourself after accepting and understanding information from external and internal sources. Knowledge is not wisdom. Wisdom is doing. It is the difference in knowing the path and walking it.

Illumination, or enlightenment, means that one has achieved total spiritual awareness. To enlighten means to fill with light, which is energy, and energy is information. To be "enlightened" simply means that someone has utilized their ability to accept and understand events and information without judgment. Although we definitely have the ability, few of us will achieve illumination, but all of us can certainly be enlightened.

We need to be aware of the plateaus we encounter when overcoming addictions and trying new things. There will be bright and encouraging periods of progress followed by slight declines and "flat" periods of little or no progress. It is wise to review what we have accomplished at that point, think about how far we have come and keep applying what we have learned. We should try to enjoy and utilize the plateaus just as much as the bright periods, rather than remain frustrated and discouraged.

You will probably want to be careful when explaining new discoveries to others. Keep in mind how difficult it is for us to understand that few things are as they appear, until we reach that point. It is often best to be an example of the discovery- not an informer. It is much more effective to explain how you cure your own health issues and live without stress and fear to someone that asks, as opposed to just providing information that contradicts popular beliefs. You are less likely to be labeled and dismissed, and we often have limited opportunities to help others before they close their minds.

It can be a huge source of frustration and cripple relationships when our understandings change and those around us refuse to consider them. It is very difficult to watch someone suffer unnecessarily when we are certain we know the solution. Try to remember that their information is serving a purpose, and they will accept new information when they are ready, when it's their time. You might be able to introduce some beneficial ideas, or it might never happen. Trust your instincts and maintain their trust.

Even if we decide not to offer help or advice, it can be difficult for those close to us to accept the changes we decide to make if they do not understand them, and they could become uncomfortable around us when doing things we no longer do. We might get left out of the loop or become less popular and it could really test our patience or cause us to question ourselves. We should try to keep vital relationships healthy and apply what we learn to strengthen them, while also accepting that the ones holding us back must change or end. You will soon be at a higher level of awareness and must know when to make room for relationships and when to take time for yourself to move forward.

The 7x Rule

A very beneficial study of memory concluded that we are seven times more likely to remember something when we write it down. Whether reading a book or an article, or even when watching a documentary, it is wise to get into the habit of taking good notes. The act of writing something down greatly increases our ability to remember because we must focus the mind and are left with a mental image of the information. Some people can see their written notes in their mind's eye when recalling information they have written down, and we have a quick and accessible reference if we forget.

The Good Stuff

It might seem discouraging when you realize that there is so much false information in the media. What does it mean if most of what we've been told is untrue? What can we believe in? Some of us comprehend that the world being shown to us is not real, but the question remains; what *is* real? It can be so confusing that the most important answers seem unattainable, and we eventually stop asking.

The encouraging news is there is just as much beneficial information available. There are countless scientists, doctors, nutritionists, researchers, and others that write incredible books, produce fascinating documentaries, operate instructive websites, and deliver informative lectures around the world. They are on the cutting edge of scientific, clinical and metaphysical research, and doing everything possible to get their proven discoveries accepted and understood, which is a difficult task when their findings contradict the deceptions the elite want us to keep believing. Industries will crumble when enough people discover that they do not need most of the products, medications and advice being sold to them.

There are some mainstream publications that report current and fascinating discoveries, such as Science and Nature magazines, but the average person does not make or have time to explore them. With some exceptions, they only report hard facts and rarely provide any logical theories that would lend understanding and explain the deeper relevance. They tend to stay grounded in the physical and some things simply cannot be physically proven; they can only be theorized or experienced. Those are the cases where we need information from the people with the best theories and experiences. You will discover some that I have found to be extremely beneficial as we progress, but there are many more and they become increasingly abundant once we begin to venture outside the corporate media box. The illusion begins to fade as we uncover the simple truths, and it gets easier to determine what *is* real.

There are some very informative Nature and science programs on corporate television; although, it is wise to remember that they are definitely on the trailing edge and completely grounded in the physical. We can find some wonderful information and fascinating new discoveries, but rarely the whole story and their real significance. They can be informative and enjoyable, but please keep in mind that all the educational channels on network and satellite/cable television are a part of mainstream media, which also means that most television history programs and documentaries are nothing more than theatrical dramatizations of the same misleading stories once fabricated for mainstream distribution.

I once saw a scientific documentary on mainstream television and they were touching on the subject of Quantum Mechanics, referring to it as, "That Q word", and implying that it was some outlandish and incomprehensible New Age theory. Then a Nobel Prize-winning scientist provided some accurate, but seemingly complicated information, which can only be comprehended after one has become familiar with the basic principles. I imagined that he probably provided some preliminary information during the filming, only to have it removed by the editor. Viewers saw Quantum Mechanics acknowledged, but most of them were likely confused and left with no understanding of its empowering significance. We can see how that same thought-limiting seed is also planted in the motion picture industry:

I recently saw the film, Men in Black, which I had previously viewed when it was released back in the year 1997. Yes, I watch some forward-thinking Hollywood productions, they are my guilty pleasure. I still enjoy kicking back in a hypnotic state and being entertained, I just view it all in a different way. I realize that I am being affected at the subconscious level, but now I'm able to identify some of the methods and applications.

There was a scene where agent J was trying out for the MIB, in which he chose to shoot a pop-up target of an unarmed human girl instead of the scary creatures the other applicants were shooting. His reasons for not shooting the scary ones were correct and quite noble, so his character gained credibility. His reason for shooting the girl was that she was carrying quantum physics books, which had to mean that she was up to something because those books were *way too advanced* for her. The message was quick, subtle and effective, and I realized that it was implanted directly into my subconscious without my awareness when I saw the film many years ago. That was not necessarily the writer's intent. We have all been conditioned to internalize and relay thought-limiting messages without any conscious awareness.

Then forward thinking and credibility came right back into play when agent K explained, "Fifteen hundred years ago we *knew* the Earth was the center of the Universe, five hundred years ago we *knew* the Earth was flat, and fifteen minutes ago you *knew* we were alone in the Universe, just imagine what we'll *know* tomorrow". That is beautifully phrased, and such unintentional and intentional combinations automatically blend deceptive and manipulative suggestions with the good stuff to ensure our acceptance.

The hidden agenda is to make us believe that Quantum Mechanics is far beyond our comprehension, and we should not give it any more thought. In fact, it is the hundred-plus year-old science that solves many of the mysteries of our Universe and limits absolutely nothing. The only new aspects are the amazing discoveries and theories that continue to expand our understanding of the unseen world, and I recalled that there were many significant scientific breakthroughs, in which theories became physically proven facts, that got a lot of attention from the early to mid-1990s, not long before MIB was filmed.

Why make Quantum Mechanics appear so intimidating throughout all parts of the media? Because it is so empowering. It can be as simple or complicated as you desire, and anyone can benefit with a little effort, time and open mind. The proven and documented basics could and should be introduced at an early age, along with several other internal technologies that would minimize the elite's ability to limit and control us.

The Internet

We have access to unlimited information thanks to the computer age and the world-wide web. It can be very beneficial or very misleading, depending on how it is used. There is false and true information, just like other sources, and we still must determine what is real. The difference is we have a search bar and can investigate almost anything with minimal time and effort. The information is not selected and presented through television, radio or textbooks, and we are in complete control of what we want to explore.

We should keep in mind that mainstream media always have their propaganda at the top of our search pages, with words and events defined by AI overviews. They have the most to hide, the most to lose, and they will spend the most money to ensure that we find the same information via the internet as we do via television and other outlets. We often must dig a little deeper and go further down the page to find what we're looking for.

And do not forget that they will lead every revolution against themselves by creating pages and sites that appear to challenge their information, but still effectively lead us away from the truth. They have become proficient at discrediting beneficial websites by bombarding the comment sections with conflicting and negative opinions. It is best to identify and disregard unproductive and dismissive comments from the trained experts that utilize calculated methods to steer us back toward the mainstream view.

It is safe and certain to state that anything we find on the internet is a result of someone somewhere that wants us to believe something. What's most important is why. Are they trying to sell us something? Products and services can be beneficial, so that's not necessarily a *bad* thing. The key is to determine if their overall intent is to empower us in some way for mutual benefit or mislead us for their benefit.

What Truth?

How can we ensure that your mind is sufficiently freed from propaganda as required to objectively consider the rest of the information herein? I believe that we can accomplish that with one undeniable example of disinformation:

Earth's solar orbit changes from circular to elliptical over time in a natural phenomenon known as eccentricity, which creates a heating and cooling cycle that completes every 100,000 years. Its surface is spinning and wobbling at 1,000 miles per hour, and its axis is tilted at 1.5 degrees toward or away from the Sun. The angle to the Sun and angle to the core of the Milky Way create a heating and cooling cycle that completes every 41,000 years. Changes in the Earth's frequency, electromagnetic field and changing solar temperatures create shorter, nested cycles of 21,000 and 11,000 years. That information was confirmed with data collected from the Greenland ice sheets and core samples from Antarctica, which reveal the temperature of the Earth over the last 420,000 years.

All those cycles and changes result in the heating and cooling cycle we experience, with a duration of approximately 30,000 years. The last ice age was approximately 15,000 years ago. During that time, we experienced extremely low temperatures and ice over a mile high covered the Northern hemisphere. Today, 15,000 years later, we have recently passed the peak of high temperatures and global cooling has begun. Global warming (and cooling) is surely real, but it's a natural process that is not caused by high carbon dioxide and methane levels. In fact, periods of higher temperatures have preceded periods of higher gas levels by 400 to 1,000 years over the last 800,000 years. Many experts believe that the other planets experience climate change, but I do not think they are driving around in cars on Mars.

That is not to say that it's okay to remove what is supposed to stay in the Earth and release it into the atmosphere by burning it. That's insane and newer methods, such as fracking for natural gas, are advertised as "safe and clean", but nothing is further from the truth. Our air, water and food are becoming increasingly toxic and it's having a huge, unnecessary impact on everything. Fossil fuels were made obsolete after Nikola Tesla discovered his free energy method, which was suppressed by J.P. Morgan and other major investors in the energy industry. Since then, countless viable and economical energy solutions have been purchased and suppressed, making oil and eventually pharmaceutical companies the most profitable businesses in the world. Obviously, changes need to be made through awareness, but there is nothing anyone could have done to cause or prevent global warming.

So, why put all the blame on us, which began back in 2006? Let's apply a method used for manufacture of consent: We were shown the *problem*: rapid climate change. We provided the *reaction*: fear for future generations. What *solution* is being proposed? A big hoax like this always has multiple purposes and money is always a factor. Carbon taxing and fuel price and tax increases are psychologically justified when associated with the looming guilt of global warming. Funding for research into this false premise cost a fortune. Under the guise of blocking sunlight, private jets flying at 15,000 feet spray heavy metals and other toxins into the atmosphere, which fall to Earth, lower our immunity and decrease our ability to reproduce. It's an effective distraction, commanding our energy to the awareness and prevention of something we cannot prevent, and another goal is to enforce limits on energy consumption.

Our indigenous ancestors understood the warming and cooling of the Earth through their history of living through cycles and changes. They also understood and foretold everything that we are experiencing today. I continue to be amazed by what was known and accomplished thousands of years ago by those “primitive” civilizations, and I'm convinced that we must learn to understand and apply the lessons that served them so well to eventually know ourselves and our purpose. After all, that was their intent.

Cool fact: After the ice age, the Great Lakes were formed as the ice melted in the depressions made by its weight, and the Earth has been slowly pushing back into place as the water is evacuated through rivers and streams. The lakes will shallow, freeze and reform as the cycle repeats.

Chapter Two

Become Aware

We thought the Earth was the center of the Universe fifteen hundred years ago, but seventeen hundred years ago we knew better. It is not disputed that the ancients had knowledge of Astronomy and Astrology thousands of years ago, so how is it possible that we thought the Earth was flat since then?

In the year 325 AD the Great Library of Alexandria, which contained over a half million scrolls, was burned by the Freemason Emperor Constantine after taking control of the Roman Catholic Church. There were no printing presses back then, everything was written on scrolls, and any copies were made by hand. Burning the library led many people to believe that all their written knowledge was lost, and some relied on their elders to educate them. That's how some of the information made it through to the present day, along with its inclusion in religion and found copies of some of the scrolls.

A group of Freemasons was also responsible for the end of the last Egyptian matriarchal society, in which the queen and other women ruled the lands. In fact, a severely misguided branch has heavily influenced many societies throughout history and continues to dominate politics, finance and the military to this day. Their goals are thought control, ethnic cleansing, property theft, a one-world government (UN), and population reduction to five hundred million people in accordance with the Georgia Guidestones.

After the death of the last noble and caring Roman emperor, Marcus Aurelius, in the year 180 AD, the original forty-five volumes of the Bible were heavily edited, finishing around the same year of 325 AD. Twenty-five were completely omitted and twenty were reduced to the single book we have today. Any honest Bible scholar will tell us that the good book is incomplete, and that is the reason for the more than one hundred different sects under the single religion of Christianity. Please ask yourself if you based your religious beliefs on what you learned from the Bible or what you were told it means.

The Bible is not for reader comprehension, it requires explanation and was intended to be confusing, misleading and difficult to believe. It was designed, along with the printing press, to bring in the "new law". I had faith and believed the mythical stories in the Bible until I reached adolescence, when the misinterpretation of Darwin's theories we were taught in school led me to not believe in the spiritual world. For years I believed only what I could physically sense to be the complete and finite Universe, until I did my own research and found the simple truth in between the myths and the skepticism.

There is truth in the Bible, but most is not for everyone to see. Much is hidden in symbolism, and the deeper meanings are open to interpretation, which was the purpose of the edits. Many conclusions can be drawn and seemingly proven from the incomplete information. True knowledge is hidden and taught to select minds, while multiple misleading versions create confusion, separation and disbelief for the uninitiated. The unedited Bible left little open to interpretation and contained empowering lessons originally assembled by Jesus and the ancient civilization known as the Essenes. We have been conditioned through Western educational systems and churches to believe that we must choose between science and spirituality, while we should be using modern science to help affirm the spiritual world.

Most religious texts take on new meaning and make more sense after we understand the use of symbolism. I once had a pleasant conversation with a college student that attended church and had just completed a course in religion. He had detailed knowledge of the stories in the Bible but was in the process of concluding that they were all just myths, and the course in religion was causing him to doubt the spiritual world, just as a high school class had done for me. Evidently, the course curriculum had not effectively addressed the symbolic meanings or attempted to interpret the underlying messages, so I asked if any of the stories would make more sense if there were deeper meanings that represented something else entirely. And what if the God in most religions is simply a personification of our unified consciousness?

It was like a switch flipped and I got to watch his mind light up. I sensed that those unbelievable stories were going to take on new meanings, and he would be forming a logical understanding of the spiritual world with his existing knowledge, along with any new information he decided to pursue.

Back in the year 325 the theft of the scrolls and the Bible edits effectively disconnected most of the population from the empowering knowledge that enabled the harmony, accomplishments and spiritual understandings of many previous civilizations. That places us at the mercy of teachers that have been misled by the inaccurate interpretations and causes many of us to stay grounded in the physical world, without any true spiritual understanding.

Believe Or Else

Skip forward almost eight hundred years, to the end of the eleventh century, and we find that many people rejected the New Testament and its Savior. By the way, most major religions have saviors, like the Buddha, Krishna, Shed, and Osiris, most with immaculate conceptions, wise men and the promise of salvation upon their acceptance. That is not to say that Jesus and the others do not exist. I am only stating that the same story has been repeated in numerous religions throughout history. As we move forward you will see that even if those leaders did not actually walk the Earth, they are either personifications of existing spiritual beings or their entities were created from the thoughts of the millions that believe in them.

What did the church do with the people that refused to accept their savior? They massacred them. The Christian Crusaders were promised salvation and eternal life for their souls if they killed all those that did not believe in Jesus Christ. The main reason the crusades ended, in that form, was the men doing the actual slaying came to realize that what they were doing was wrong. We see that in modern times when U.S. and allied soldiers become aware and realize why they are sent to other countries under the guise of peace, liberty and security. Appearances change, but the reason remains the same. The crusades were never truly about religion or acceptance, and our modern wars are not about protection from terrorists that hate us because of our way of life. The purpose has always been control.

Religion

Ancient civilizations had unlimited knowledge of our physical and spiritual worlds, and their wisdom helped me to realize the difference between religion and spirituality. Religions are words written by men to communicate their spiritual understandings. Spirituality is our understanding and awareness of the unseen world and the Divine Intellect that is the Source of all creation. I came to believe that what is most important is not what can be seen, but that which connects all things. We are not separate from each other or anything in our Universe, but most of us have lost our awareness of the connection.

There is much beauty and truth in religion, but there is also much confusion and separation. In the beginning there was no religion, there were no rules and regulations and people had universal spiritual understandings. Religion was introduced as a means to teach but became a means to control through division of thought, which created our *duality* (judgment of good or evil).

Within most major religions, a large majority of the followers concentrate on the surface meanings and give their energy to an external source (God) that is separate from us, and a small minority realize the deeper truths and understand that the Source (god) exists within all physical matter and on all metaphysical planes. That knowledge allows us to see the true meaning of the phrase, "God is in everyone and everything". What do you think Jesus meant when he said that we are all gods, but do not know it, and what did the Buddha intend when he said that we all have his potential within us?

When we take a closer look at ancient societies, we discover that the teachings of most ancient cultures and religions are very similar, and that includes the early Christians, who were known as the Gnostics, taken from the word, *gnosis*, which means *esoteric knowledge*. These societies originated in different parts of the world with no physical means of communication during different eras throughout history and shared the same conclusions.

They realized that this is a temporary place for the eternal soul to experience and master emotions, know itself in every way and achieve karmic balance. They had detailed knowledge of reincarnation because those things are rarely accomplished in one lifetime, and they believed that we are all part of a single source of consciousness, which manifests our reality and creates the physical Universe from our collective consciousness and thought.

Think about that for a moment... Christians and every other major religious group shared the same knowledge of the unseen world and believed in reincarnation. What if the true meaning of being "born again" is simply to be born again in this physical world? What if "accepting" a savior simply means to accept their teachings and the process of life? I'm not insisting that is accurate, but the belief that one religion is *right* and all the others are *wrong* is definitely not true, and easy to see past once you look.

The Serpent

All ancient cultures were fascinated by the snake's ability to shed its skin and consume the toxins in the prey it poisoned. They realized that the peptides (proteins) in the body, venom and blood of the snake had beneficial properties and perfected elixirs to remedy conditions, raise immunity and improve longevity. They also used the skin of the snake to heal cuts and other surface wounds. Their reverence evolved into worship, and the serpent became the foundation of every major religion we have today.

It began at least seventy thousand years ago, as evidenced by the serpent carvings found in a recently discovered cave in Botswana, Africa. The Rainbow Serpent in Australia, which split off from the rest of the world fifty thousand years ago, reveals that they either worshiped the serpent before that time or developed it on their own. Japanese and Chinese texts reveal that their cultures worshiped the dragon at least seven thousand years ago, and serpent worship greatly intensified in every part of the world around 1,000 BC. Countless hieroglyphs, carvings, paintings, and statues found in Egypt, Europe, India, Greece, and the Americas affirm that every culture and religious group once highly revered snakes.

We only need to open our perception and look at our churches, religious texts and common symbols to see that snakes are everywhere. The medical industry's symbol consists of two snakes, coiled around a staff with wings and a ball of light at the top, and was taken from the Hindu symbol for enlightenment. The purpose is to subconsciously replace holistic health with medication. The serpents symbolize our feminine and masculine energies, and the staff symbolizes our spine. These Kundalini energies are coiled around the base of the spine three and a half times and rise to the crown as the chakras (energy centers) are opened along the path to illumination, which is symbolized by the wings and ball of light.

In Greek mythology, the serpent's duality is symbolized by the two types of blood that came from the snake-haired head of Medusa. One would cure you and one would kill you. We have the Buddhist story of the Buddha subduing the fiery serpent and we can find many statues, carvings and paintings where he is holding a chalice full of serpents. There is also the Islamic story of Muhammad being cured by the serpent worshipers. In England, another name for the king was Pin Dragon. Pin means head and dragon means serpent, so he was known as the Head Serpent. Hak Pin Hill at Avebury, England has a massive collection of stones in the shape of a snake's head. Hak means snake, so the name means Snake Head Hill, and Eve was derived from Ave for the story of the Garden of Eden and original sin (knowledge).

The Gnostics (early Christians) worshiped the serpent until around 900 BC, when their perception changed, and the new Christians began to eliminate serpent worship around the world. St. Patrick, St. Paul and St. Michael traveled far and wide to slay the dragon, which became symbolic of Satan.

Jesus was referred to as the Good Serpent in Gnostic times, and his crucifixion was equated to the Brazen Serpent of Moses, "Ye shall be held up as the brazen serpent in the wilderness". The people in the wilderness had been bitten by snakes and were sure to die. Moses asked God what to do and was instructed to raise up the brazen serpent on the cross and tell everyone to look at it. The people were instantly cured of their snakebites as those that saw Jesus on the cross were instantly cured of their sins.

The story of Gabriel coming down to help Mary have a child originated from a Gnostic tradition, in which the serpent came down and joined with Mary when she was only eighteen months old. Jesus was also known as the Serpent King, and early images symbolizing him were of a serpent on the cross, which seems to explain the meaning of his skin (the shroud) left in the tomb in the resurrection story and possibly solves the mystery of the contents of the Holy Grail. The red and white (blood and body) mixed in the chalice are likely symbolic of the snake's blood and venom, the original elixir of life.

It is common knowledge that modern chemists are utilizing snake venom and blood in beneficial ways but how were the ancients able to do it so long ago and how did they know about the different types of venom? Hemotoxic venom affects blood cells and tissue, and there are two types: anticoagulant and coagulant. Some of their elixirs thinned the blood and some helped it to clot. Neurotoxic venom affects the nervous system, and various elixirs were formulated for pain relief, stress and recreational use.

Some venoms contain combinations of neurotoxins and hemotoxins, and they were able to utilize them as well. Many "primitive" civilizations around the world knew how to heal, boost their immunity and extend their lives with the help of the serpent. Old West films and the media portray it as a scam, but snake oil was a legitimate healing elixir that was widely used in England, the U.S. and other parts of the world. It only became a novelty after Barnum and Bailey made and sold it in front of audiences, and its sale ended at the Prohibition because it contained alcohol. It obviously did not come back by popular demand as well as alcohol, but snake oils and associated products are still medicinally used in many parts of the world today.

Another reason snakes were worshiped is their resemblance to one of the main archetypes we see in the altered states of consciousness achieved during deep meditation. *Archetype* has multiple meanings; in this context it means *an image from the collective unconscious; an inherited memory represented in the mind by a universal symbol and observed in dreams and meditation.* This is the same archetype associated with our DNA and the life-force energy wave form. There are periods in the Earth's cycles when higher amounts of energy are drawn to Earth and that wave form can be seen by everyone- not just clairvoyants, when concentrating on a section of blue sky. We are in one of those periods now and you can perform the following to see for yourself:

Go outside and stand or sit in an open area on a sunny day and select a large, cloudless section of blue sky, without any glare from the sun. Hold your attention on that area, but do not focus your eyes, just gaze and allow your peripheral vision to balance. You will begin to see balls of streaking light, and they will become more detailed until you eventually see the coiled formation of energy. It is the shape of your DNA; it's the shape of the serpent.

Paganism

Paganism is the worship of the stars, planets, elements, and Nature practiced by ancient Egyptian, Hopi, Mayan, and other indigenous cultures, and is a way to acknowledge, honor and appreciate the physical parts of the Universe that permeate and sustain physical life. It became associated with evil and satanism, along with serpent worship and alchemy, and we often only hear about the dark side, such as blood sacrifice, in order to hide the wisdom of those civilizations. Paganism is actually the most widely practiced religion in the world today because it is unwittingly practiced in all religions.

Pagan rituals, doctrines and symbols have been skillfully integrated into every religion, government and military body over thousands of years, by the same organizations that made their origins appear evil, so we will blindly worship or follow without the empowering knowledge that would prevent our participation. For example, the catholic/christian cross was derived from the solstice and equinox division lines on the ancient Zodiac Calendar. Originally it had a circle around the crossing point, marked with angle increments, and was used like a protractor to measure and map the stars and planets.

Wedding rings are a pagan tradition and symbolize the rings of Saturn, circumcision is a ritual for marking pagan males and gravestones immortalize the pagan soul. Baptism is a pagan ritual, in which one is submerged in holy water to symbolize the renewal of life as the rain replenishes the Earth. Heaven is actually the pagan word for the galactic bodies of the Universe and the word, amen, used at the end of prayer, was taken from the Egyptian pharaoh known as Amen-Ra. In ancient Egypt, the Goddess Isis was the personification of wisdom and Ra was the Sun God. When the Hebrews traveled from Egypt to the Middle East, the indigenous people there worshiped the God Saturn El. The eventual merging of those three gods became the name of that land: Isis-Ra-El, or Israel. Judaism is based around the worship of Saturn, and the day of worship was SATURday. Worship on SUNday originated with the ancient Egyptian practice of worshiping the Sun.

Pagan symbols are almost everywhere, and we rarely notice the abundance or realize the psychological effect, until we become consciously aware of their existence. Most of the symbols on government buildings, churches, monuments, military uniforms, corporate logos, and currency are masonic, and all have specific meaning and purpose. Much is learned from researching the symbols on your cash and coins. The biggest, in-plain-sight example is the Statue of Liberty, which is a tribute to the Greek Goddess Athena.

Ancient pagan societies believed that life taken at a specific time and place, in a specific manner, was a sacrifice and there are many horrific examples of that ritual in modern times. In the year 2003 the U.S. began bombing the city of Baghdad on March 20th and continued operation Shock and Awe until May 1st. Those are the same days of the pagan ritual in which they give blood to the Earth. The massacre at Waco, Texas and the Oklahoma City bombing took place, in different years within that ritual period, on April 17th, and the W.T.C. controlled demolitions "occurred" on their sacrificial day of September 11th.

There are *good* and *bad* branches of Freemasons, and the latter have capitalized on numerous major wars by controlling the resulting debts, and that includes the U.S. Revolutionary War and Civil War. Ulysses S. Grant went from the status of private to commander of the Union army from April of 1861 to May of 1864 because his father was Master Mason Jesse Grant. His presidential cabinet housed eight Freemasons, including Alfonzo Taft, father of William Taft and ancestor of sex scandal distraction artist, Bill Clinton. Presidents are not elected; they are selected for specific purposes.

It is no secret that George Washington was a Freemason, and we can find paintings of him with the same symbol found at all masonic temples. Obviously, the "G" does not represent George, Georgia or St. Germaine. One logical explanation I have found is that it is symbolic of *giant*, as the original meaning is *one that comes from above*, which was described in ancient hieroglyphs of beings coming down from the heavens. Most likely it is simple numerology, in which G is 7 and proclaims spiritual perfection. Every president was or is directly linked to the Freemasons or the Illuminati. The two were re-merged by the Weishaupt and Rothschild families in the year 1780, which allowed the Illuminati use of the masonic temples. Their goal was and is to control the human race by delivering us from all spirituality.

There were two presidents that developed either a heavy conscience or an increased awareness and attempted to print their own currency to break away from the Central Bank or the Federal Reserve, which is a private bank, owned and controlled by the Rothschild family. They were Abraham Lincoln and John F. Kennedy. There was another that spoke out against them, a former actor and spokesperson for one of the world's largest corporations prior to his political career. His name was Ronald Reagan.

Secret Societies

The men and events I describe are not to be feared, but they also cannot be ignored or denied. All that is required for us to overcome their influence is to change our perception, but we cannot do that until we become aware of our true surroundings. The only action to initially take is exploring and utilizing the information they desperately keep from us until we have the wisdom to become less dependent, but that is not possible until we become consciously aware of the control they have over our subconscious through the media, schools, religion, and politics. We cannot continue to blindly follow, worship or dismiss their doctrines, rituals and symbols and expect to see beyond them; although, we should not become obsessed with what they are doing and give away our emotional energy, which fuels the fire.

There are groups of people that have been working behind the scenes for thousands of years to manipulate every aspect of humanity. Some have vast esoteric knowledge to practice and accomplish the very things we dismiss as superstitions and impossibilities. They are known as secret societies, and some of them could be viewed as *good* and even necessary. In fact, most members and followers of the secret societies viewed as *evil* actually have good intent and believe that what they are doing is best. The strings are pulled from the top and the puppets are born or recruited into the ranks, where they are monitored during their education to determine what they will be told and how to utilize their energy.

For example, there was a religious secret society that tested its members after they reached a certain level by instructing them to spit on the cross. Those that refused were praised and commended and then utilized to achieve the society's goals without any knowledge of their actual intentions. Those that consented were also praised and commended but were initiated into the higher positions of knowledge and power, where they were made aware of the society's true purpose and intent only when necessary.

Very few people would participate if they knew the underlying purposes and intentions of some of these organizations, and that is the same reason government and military personnel are conditioned to blindly follow orders without the need to know under the guise of interests in national security.

We also see this in almost every educational system in the world. Those that can absorb information without question and reproduce it during tests become politicians or qualified professionals, and those that utilize their common sense to apply logic and question the information are reduced and limited. The irony is the qualified professionals are also severely reduced and limited, and that is the actual meaning of the word. The legal definition of the verb, *qualify*, is *to reduce or limit*, and that is also listed in standard dictionaries after *to give suitable qualities* and *to furnish with knowledge*.

If someone is qualified and licensed to practice something, they have been reduced and limited to the methods of the industry that gave the suitable qualities and furnished the knowledge. If they deviate from the approved methods and practices of their industry, they will be disqualified (lose their license). The result is many bright minds are reduced and limited to achieve the goals of their industry without any knowledge of better methods that would decrease the industry's profits and any realization of their actual intent to maintain wealth, power and control. The current legal industry could not exist without misguiding those within it and we are worth much more to the medical industry sick instead of well.

An example of the power of propaganda is the misinterpretation of the concept of *communism*, which intends a *commonwealth*, which means that all people equally share the abundant wealth of their country- not that everyone will be poor. What has been utilized in other countries and what we have been shown has even the poorest people supporting capitalism, inequality and the super-rich, who keep them pacified by continuously dangling the "you could be one of us someday" carrot in front of them.

The legal definition of the word, *lie*, is *proper* and *fitting*, so if you agree that something is a "lie" in Court, you have stated that it's true. *Understand* is legally defined as *stand under*, which translates to *consent to jurisdiction*.

All the *citizens*, protesting the fact that a *corporation* is a *person*, need to check the dictionary. Person is also the class of U.S. citizen created with the Fourteenth Amendment in the year 1868. A *political person* is classified as a corporation and unwittingly surrenders their human rights, in order to participate in commerce, in what is known as the Strawman Illusion.

Contracting to be a citizen also places us under the jurisdiction of the British Grand Lodge Masonic System known as Statutory Court, where *as king* was changed to *asking*. A *natural person* (living soul, human being) is a king in *Court* (palace, castle) and demands are made as king, while a *political person* (corporation, state) can only make requests by asking.

The only difference between a *state* and an *estate* is the "e", and both are corporations. Two political persons (states) can unite to form a nation, which is how a secret society has a seat at the U.N. without representing an actual land. The Secretary of State is the executor of the second Cestui Que Vie Trust, a negotiable instrument created with your birth *certificate* (a paper establishing an ownership claim) and incorporated with your social security number. The first Cestui Que Vie Trust is the Testimony Trust, created with the Constitution, in which you are the beneficiary, the state is the executor and public officials are the trustees. Statutory jurisdiction can only be enforced on states, but we must know how to verbally and formally make the distinction that we are natural persons- not citizens. All law is now written or spoken contract law, and any form of consensual citizenship executes the contracts created with previous documents and subjects you to jurisdiction.

Control

The Freemasons gained control in ancient Egypt, expanded to Greece and then Rome, where they still control the Holy Roman Empire. Yes, the pope is a Freemason. They took control of England, Ireland and France in the thirteenth century, but did not have to take control in America because they were in power from the beginning. Why does every world leader kneel before the pope and kiss his hand? Why would any U.S. president be knighted by the queen of England? Because that is the chain of command.

There are three sovereign city-states that control almost every aspect of our world through religion, finance and the military. They have their own flags, operate above and beyond all jurisdiction, and are symbolized by the triple crown formed when the city of Babylon was divided into three parts.

Religion is controlled by the first city-state; Vatican City, Rome (the dragon). The Freemasons there were responsible for the theft of the scrolls, editing the Bible, the Gregorian Calendar, and the Christian Crusades. Regardless of your denomination, a Baptismal Certificate is sent to the Vatican after you are baptized, which creates the third Cestui Que Vie Trust. The three CQV Trusts claim legal ownership of your property, body and soul. The Vatican controls the second city-state; London, England (the wild beast), which controls the third city-state; Washington, DC (the false prophet).

London, England is the financial control, and we must go back to the year 1213 to see how that came about: Pope Innocent III planned to control all the lands of the world under their doctrine, in which he is the Vicar of Christ. He claimed that he was the owner of all lands and people on behalf of Jesus, until he returns, and demanded that King John surrender England, Ireland and France. The king refused but was excommunicated from the church and told he would suffer eternal damnation. King John was a very religious man and decided to hand over the lands in the contract known as the Treaty of Verona, which led to the signing of Magna Carta in the year 1215.

Great Britain became an agent for the pope and the Holy Roman Empire and began to gain control of other lands by instigating, manipulating and financing wars from both sides. Most governments could not repay the loans and were forced to pledge the future labor of their people, convince them that labor was worth much less and tax their income.

King George, who was also the king of France, financed the American Revolutionary War via French bankers and worked with the Founding Fathers to install a central government and tie the people to a debt that could not be paid. On January 22nd, 1783, Congress ratified a contract for the repayment of twenty-one loans received by the U.S. from 1778 to 1782. Congress met again in Philadelphia on May 14th, 1787 to revise the Articles of Confederation because the country was bankrupt. Twelve state delegates approved the Constitution on September 17th, 1787, in which the states became *constitutors*, which means *responsible for the payment of someone else's debt by simple agreement*. The states were then liable, but the people were not because the Constitution was not put to them for a vote.

On August 4th, 1790, an act was passed that made provisions for the payment of the debt of the United States, which abolished the states and created federal districts that were each assigned a portion of the debt. The original State Constitutions were also never submitted to the people for a vote, so the state governments submitted new constitutions to the people for approval, which unwittingly bound them and us to the debts owed to Great Britain. That is the foundation of the Strawman Illusion, in which our future labor is pledged via our birth certificates, which are grouped into bonds and traded as stocks, while we are legally regarded as *persons* (corporations, states, citizens, residents, government-created fictions, collateral, and chattel), instead of living human beings, unless we make the distinction.

The only thing backing our currency is our future labor. All our gold was taken to help pay the interest on the past-due loans in the year 1933. The U.S. Federal Government had formed itself into a corporation in the year 1871. It is no longer a sovereign nation, it's a corporation, like SEARS or GE, except it is in bankruptcy and struggling to pay the interest on past-due loans. Therefore, the national debt and most causes of inflation are only hoaxes that originated on paper and are now fabricated on computer keypads. They are necessary to support the ruse and pay the bankers' bad gambling debts.

Golden fact: The banking system originated with the goldsmiths, who quickly realized that they did not need the gold to lend notes, which led to fractional banking, in which only fiat money is transferred electronically.

Washington, DC became the military control, which is the actual reason the U.S.A. now has more than eight hundred active military bases in other countries around the world. The plan is to hand them over to the United Nations in the year 2030 and have a one-world government and new-world order. That is not a theory, it's a fact, and ignoring their intentions is exactly what got us to this critical stage of awareness. The U.S.A. signed the Declaration on Open Government for the implementation of the U.N. 2030 Agenda for Sustainable Development Goals on September 27, 2015. The agenda appears to be in our best interests, but their main goal is to create an unprecedented level of control and dependence.

What it's going to take is for more of the people unwittingly supporting and participating in the plan to become aware of what they are doing, just as the Christian Crusaders did. An encouraging example of that necessity was evidenced in the year 2005 after Hurricane Katrina in New Orleans when National Guard soldiers were ordered to confiscate all the weapons from the homes in the affected area. Most of them acted upon their instincts and refused to follow those orders out of loyalty to the people.

Our knowledge is our power, and the elite entities behind the military can only succeed if they are able to control it. It seems that the only way for us to "win" is to quit playing their game.

Mark Of The Beast

The Strawman Illusion is a form of *Maritime Admiralty* (the law of water; *banking* law), in which you are a *vessel* born into the *sea* of commerce from your mother's birth *canal*, making you a *product* of commerce. The *docktor* waives the docking fee in exchange for your birth rights. The Washington Monument is actually a sea-level obelisk that infers America is under water and therefore subject to Maritime Admiralty.

Common Law is the Law of the Land and there is only one: *We cannot breach the peace or cause injury by infringing on another living soul's life, liberty or property*. All other "laws" are statutes, based on preventing those things (300,000 federal and countless state), and their purpose is to control you and collect revenue. There is no crime unless the Common Law is broken and only corporations can violate statutes. That is how O.J. secretly avoided conviction in the statutory (state's) case. Only a civil case or warrant where the injured party or a relative filed a *claim* with the magistrate has any legal merit on land.

I once believed that all attorneys and judges must know these things and be part of the scam, until I realized how secret societies operate and control curriculum. Some do know, and some get out when they realize who they are really working for, while a few attempt to balance the system from within.

That is also the case when IRS agents learn that they actually work for a foreign, private banker and mandatory federal income taxing cannot be enforced upon natural persons, but we voluntarily contract to pay it via our employment and voter registrations. The cruel irony is that our ancestors believed they fought a war to stop paying taxes to Great Britain but that is exactly where all federal tax revenue goes. Duties, imposts, excises, and other taxes provide too much revenue to run the "government" (private, foreign interests) and the excess is given away in foreign aid. The IRS is simply a collection agency for the London loan sharks, and the Revolutionary War was a methodical scheme to establish a system of financial control.

CIA, FBI, DHS, NSA, FEMA, and all other agents, who believe they are working for the people of a sovereign nation, actually work for those individual corporations, in which the corporation named the UNITED STATES OF AMERICA owns stock. By the way, do you know of any corporation that would allow the general public to select its president? Notice that a corporation's name is always spelled with all capital letters. Now look at your driver's license, social security card, payment statements, or any document where your name is used to participate in commerce. That name is a government-created, fictitious entity and your corporate title- not you.

The details of our legal/economic system are beyond the scope of this book; although, the basics are necessary to realize *what* we are not on the path to understanding *who* we are. So, we will conclude this section by clarifying the extent and impact of this blatantly fraudulent scheme and move forward. If we are charged with a crime and there is no injured party or filed claim, we have not broken the Common Law, we are volunteering to accept statutory charges by consenting that we are Fourteenth Amendment Citizens (states).

How do visitors from other countries declare diplomatic immunity from statutory law? They declare they are not citizens. We are born with that right and choice, as stated in the Universal Declaration of Human Rights, but we actually forfeit all of our human rights as citizens. Previously all human beings forced to go to war or flee the country could have avoided being drafted by rescinding their citizenship and any other existing contracts. Currently the for-profit prisons are full of natural persons unjustly convicted of non-injury statutes because they do not know *who* they are.

We all bare the mark of the wild beast (London), a number. It is the serial number of your stock, located on the back of your social security card in red (blood), and represents your body and name (nombre), which is your mark... "Sign your name or make your mark". In law, natural persons do not have surnames, and your full name is the title of your corporation (strawman).

So, your name is the mark of the beast, and naming people and things is an effective means to infer and support separation (divide and conquer). It creates the ultimate forms of identity theft and separation anxiety. Again, we are not separate from anything in our Universe, and that is why most monasteries do not use names. They understand the necessity of establishing and maintaining the truth that we are one, and the dangers of forgetting.

Separation is also implied and supported by pride. Pride, at its very best, should only be associated with accomplishments- not something we are born into. National pride, racial pride, religious pride, gender pride, and even team pride are toxic notions that create a host of ill will, competition and the false belief that we are different from each other. The empowering truth is we are not names, products or collateral. We are living souls that have been deceived into believing that we must earn our right to life and unwittingly volunteer to be ruled by false government under the jurisdiction of British Courts.

Darkest Before Dawn

Most people are aware of what took place in history but unaware of how and why. I have described a dark part of our true surroundings that we allow to manifest by remaining unaware. There are certainly those that are more responsible than others, but we must all begin to accept our responsibility. Fool me once, shame on us, fool me twice, shame on me. The control systems are not full of people attempting to do harm, they are comprised of people that believe what they are doing is best. If you can convince enough people that up is down, left is right and wrong is right, you can fool most of the people most of the time. The result is the experts that make or advise our most important decisions are often sincere but sincerely wrong. Everyone's good intentions will be properly directed as we become aware.

I stated in the foreword that the majority would likely find difficulty in accepting this information. That is because acceptance is the final stage of an often-uncomfortable process that can include denial, anger, bargaining, guilt, and depression. When dealing with the truth, what is initially uncomfortable will eventually be empowering.

We might compare it to losing a sore tooth. It hurts before you pull it, it really hurts when you pull it, then it's always much better after the process. If we just ignore the problem, we might become numb to the pain, but the issue remains. We must go through the process of acceptance because not knowing the truth is the root cause of all our pain, stress and fear.

The discomfort level is always high with "180-degree information". If I told you that I can fly, you would just laugh it off and no one gets offended. If I provide a familiar, conflicting opinion, we can agree to disagree without too much feather ruffling. However, if I state something that appears to be opposite of your beliefs, but your instincts tell you is true, then there is an uncomfortable internal conflict. So, your defense mechanisms kick in and out comes denial, which becomes a prison for your mind until you overcome it and any remaining stages required to complete the process of acceptance.

It might not seem like much consolation at this point, but you will soon realize that everything in the world must balance, and every seemingly evil being and event have purpose and are divine in nature because they all originate from the same Divine Source. That understanding allows us to experience compassion without anger, forgiveness without resentment and love without fear. Most of us recognize this purpose, necessity and beauty in Nature, with the relationship between predator and prey, but it can be difficult to relate it to our existence until we realize that we are all here for a reason, and sometimes that reason is simply to balance. Harmony in Nature is physically evidenced by species replacement, in which an extinct species is always replaced by an emerging species of the same vibrational frequency.

We should never fear what dark secret societies attempt to accomplish at the spiritual level. All esoteric practices and rituals are powered by intent. Love-based intentions are very powerful and fear-based intentions are much less powerful, which is why those attempting to do harm must work together in large groups to have a limited impact. That is also why they desperately control the physical world and our perception of the unseen world.

A fact not fit for the faint of heart is that over five thousand monasteries in China and India have been invaded, and more than a million monks were massacred over the last sixty years. They were self-supportive, loving and caring people that had little or nothing of monetary value, posed no threat to anyone, and often focused on projecting a beneficial reality for the rest of the world. It seems that the only purpose anyone could have for harming them would be a desperate attempt to create an imbalance, swing the scales and level the playing field.

Always remember that you can take a single candle into a dark room and fill it with light, but you cannot take any amount of darkness into a room full of light and fill it with darkness, so be the light.

appo deepo bhava

Chapter Three

Ancient Wisdom & Modern Science

I became curious and began to study politics, economics and religion after changing circumstances in my life afforded the opportunity. I journeyed down many rabbit holes until I discovered the truth about those systems and decided to focus on determining what is real. I turned my attention to science, Nature and the Universe, which led me to Quantum Mechanics, where I noticed that almost every book, article and documentary included some version of the same statement, "Modern science is only affirming what the ancients knew thousands of years ago". So, after I was comfortable with the physical aspect of the scientific information, I decided to find out what that meant, and maybe get ahead of the physical discoveries in modern science. What exactly had they been affirming and what was yet to be affirmed?

It was a good move, my best ever, and I have yet to look back. I found wisdom, beauty and power far beyond my imagination. It seems logical to assume that we are more advanced because of our current technologies, but the truth is many ancient civilizations did not need the devices and machinery we have today. They had knowledge of the correct frequencies and methods required to communicate and manifest, and we only need our technologies today because we lost that knowledge.

Heavy Lifting

One of the best physical examples of ancient manifestation is the Great Pyramid of Giza. Any honest engineer or associated expert will tell us that they do not know how it was built, and we do not have the technology to build one today. The popular story that thousands of workers labored over many decades does not explain how it was accomplished because it cannot be physically explained or accomplished.

The Great Pyramid contains over two and a half million blocks of limestone that weigh from two to seventy tons each, all fitted together with consistent joints of less than one-fifteenth of an inch. The joint material is extremely fine and strong and cannot be chemically defined. The base of the pyramid covers over thirteen acres, and its volume is approximately ninety-million cubic feet, which is enough masonry to build thirty Empire State buildings. Each of the triangular sides has two sides and a total area of five and a half acres, sloped at an exact fifty-one-degree angle with a finished height of 454 feet. It is simply not physically possible for any number of workers or modern equipment to collect, shape, move, and precisely place limestone blocks weighing up to 140,000 pounds. However, it was obviously accomplished, which leads us to the questions; who is more advanced and what are these lost technologies?

The materials, construction and geographic location reveal the intended purpose of the pyramid. It is not a tomb and no remains were found. There is evidence of chemical reactions and salt being used for levitation. The king's and queen's chambers have channels (vents) leading to them that produce a pitch tuned to the Earth's vibrational frequency, regardless of the air volume.

The Great Pyramid was covered with seamless, white, crystallized stone. All three are constructed of limestone and granite, which are the last two stages before crystallization, the most organized form of matter. There is a limestone aqua fir below the pyramids for increased conductivity that was fed by the Nile River, until it migrated from the area over thousands of years. That migration process and modern erosion dating technologies reveal that the pyramids and Great Sphinx were actually built around 10,490 BC.

A pyramid's construction naturally gathers ambient energy, especially when properly shaped and aligned. These are located on one of the seven Earth chakra sites, where the Earth receives and transforms its energy, and aligned with the stars of Orion’s Belt. Today, depleted and without the river charging the aqua fir, the energy is still sensed and very powerful.

The Great Pyramid of Giza was an ambient energy transformer, manifested for the benefit of the entire planet long before the Egyptian's arrived, when those in the king's and queen's chambers were able to achieve accelerated healing and inter-dimensional (astral) travel. I cannot find another logical purpose for the massive effort within the evidence, other than a method to capture, transform and distribute energy.

The Error In Time

Early civilizations did not have our distractions and paid extremely close attention to their natural surroundings. They regarded the material universe as one of the noblest works of Divine Intellect and knew that understanding, respecting and appreciating Nature would enable them to live in harmony and eventually realize the purpose of our existence. What we perceive as naive worship was often a formal form of gratitude and ancient societies took nothing for granted. All great minds throughout history, such as Plato, Aristotle and the ever-cynical Socrates, paid homage to the spirits of Nature.

With the reintegration of science and spirituality, we now know that the electromagnetic forces of stars, planets and the elements are semiconscious beings, which are directly affected by our individual thought and behavior. Ancient civilizations around the world understood that and acted accordingly.

The most obvious examples of ancient wisdom are the calendars and science of Astrology created with their knowledge of Astronomy. They lived in harmony with the cycles of the Earth, Sun and Moon until our current, twelve-month Gregorian Calendar and the first mechanical clock were imposed on the indigenous people by Pope Gregory XIII in the year 1582.

It is known as the Error in Time because it made time something external that we must watch and obey and inhibits harmony by keeping us off balance and out of synchronicity with Nature. The ancient Mayan prophet, Pacal Votan, wrote, "If humanity wishes to save itself from biospheric destruction, it must return to living in natural time", so let's look at their natural calendars:

Long ago I asked myself why there are thirteen new moons each year, but only twelve months, then gave it no more thought, until I asked myself why we have daylight savings time and kept exploring both questions until I accepted a truth that I did not want to believe. Our original calendar consisted of thirteen *moonths*, with four full weeks, 28 days and new moons always on *Moonday*, in sync with the Moon cycle and therefore in sync with the Earth and all other cycles. The Mayans called it the Short Count Calendar, and the natural simplicity allowed our ancestors to maintain *harmonium* (balance).

The Julian "solar" Calendar, implemented by Julius Caesar in 46 BCE, and the more accurate Gregorian Calendar consist of twelve months, with broken weeks, 28, 30 and 31 days, and February must have 29 days every four years to make it mathematically sound. Why would they devote so much time and energy to replacing such a perfect system with an imperfect calendar, which can never be in complete synchronicity with the solar cycle? Because an unbalanced, out-of-sync population is vulnerable and easy to control.

Furthermore, why does the general population use a twelve-hour clock, with am/pm, but the military uses a twenty-four-hour clock? What other purpose does daylight savings time serve? An hour of daylight is not magically gained with the process. A popular belief is that it was established for farmers, but they actually lobbied against the change at the time and still oppose. They lose an hour of light in the mornings and must rush crops to market, and livestock is routinely affected by altering habitual schedules.

The actual reason given to the public to get it accepted was to conserve electricity. It was introduced by Benjamin Franklin, George Hudson and William Willett in the year 1784, but not implemented until the year 1916, in Germany, and in the U.S. in 1918. The U.S. Department of Transportation initiated a study in the year 1975, in which they intended to prove that our total coal/electricity consumption would decrease one percent from March to April, but a year later there was no decrease as more electricity was used in the morning due to the lack of daylight. You cannot rob Peter to pay Paul.

The cycle in which the tilt of the Earth changes our angle to the stars is called the Precession of the Equinoxes, the Great Year and the Mayan Long Count Calendar. It is the recurring pattern of the stages of our civilization: Iron, Bronze, Silver, and Golden. The total duration of 25,625 years is divided into five periods of 5,125 years for the elements; Air, Fire, Water, Earth, and Ether, which permeates and sustains the other elements.

December 21st, 2012 was the end of the fourth element period, Earth, which began in 3113 BC, and we are now in the fifth and final period, Ether, which ends in the year 7137 AD. Each element period is divided into thirteen periods of 394 or 395 years called baktuns. The thirteenth and final baktun, which began in 1618 and ended in 2012, was the Triumph of Materialism and the Time of Great Forgetting. The Mayans accurately foretold that many would lose awareness of their true connection to Nature and domination would become the ego-driven ambition of the civilized world.

They understood that cycles and stars are maps and mirrors of what takes place on Earth and knew how to view and read them with incredible detail and accuracy. Most of us have been convinced that such things are impossible or mere superstition, while some still benefit from that wisdom.

The good news is we are now in a time of awakening, the beginning of the end of our duality, and we are steadily moving toward the balance between emotional and rational (feminine and masculine) energies.

Suppression Of The Feminine

We all have feminine and masculine energies, which are *metaphysical* (beyond physical) and actually have little to do with gender or sex. They are also known as the Yin and the Yang. Feminine energy is associated with the right hemisphere of the brain and is emotional, creative, imaginative, intuitive, conceptual, heuristic, empathetic, figurative, irregular, and focuses on the big picture. Masculine energy is associated with the left hemisphere and is rational, analytical, logical, repetitive, organized, scientific, detached, literal, sequential, and focuses on the details.

We move in and out of balance with these energies, as a society, as we travel through the Cycle of Ages (Long Count Calendar), where the Golden Ages are times of holistic thinking. It is possible for an individual to balance these energies by opening and cleansing the chakra system, and I will provide some insight into that later. Now we will look at the effects of our current deficiency of feminine energy, which is made worse by physically and psychologically suppressing those that have the strongest natural connection.

We have seen many triumphs for women in modern times, while we still see so much unfairness. Any time we chart something within a cycle, we find many ups and downs along the overall progress line. We have come very far since the "rule of thumb", which originally meant that a man should not beat a woman with a switch that had a larger diameter than his thumb. Progress will continue for thousands of years, passing the balance between masculine and feminine energies, until it peaks at the next matriarchal society, which will have opposite issues due to a natural deficiency of masculine energy.

Men formed a secret society to eventually overthrow the last matriarchal society in Egypt around 1570 BCE and began systematically suppressing women in an attempt to suppress everyone's feminine energy, which was also done through their teachings and other resulting misinterpreted teachings and religions. One example is the extreme misinterpretation of the "dress code" Muhammad advised in the Qur'an. He only stated that we should cover our naked bodies; nothing specific and nothing about women covering their heads. This is what happens when we rely on others to translate knowledge and inform us; they often transpose the information to suit their needs.

The Bible states that we have a heavenly father, which is true if we think of him as a personification of the masculine energy, but what about our heavenly mother? They even went as far as to say that God created man in his image and woman was created from man. An ongoing movement was initiated to force *man*kind into a left-brain *men*tality, isolating us from our emotions and nurturing energies.

Over time healers, shamans and psychics were replaced with science, numbers and linear thinking. We lost our bond with Nature and with each other, forgetting that every individual act and thought affect the whole. Our society teaches that we should always feel happy, and something is wrong with us when we are sad, so we take medications and find other ways to suppress our emotions without fully experiencing them, learning from them and allowing their purpose to be served by mastering them.

Feminine energy is the foundation of the human condition and the Divine Matrix of the Universe. Without it, we are overly systematic and easily controlled. We lose our creativity, intuition, empathy, and our ability to see the big picture. We are unwittingly ruled by the ego mind and tend to believe that everything is separate and scarce in lieu of accepting that everything is connected and abundant.

Darwinism

"As on the theory of natural selection an interminable number of intermediate forms must have existed... Why do we not see these linking forms all around us? Why is not every geological formation charged with such links? We meet with no such evidence, and this is the most obvious and forcible of the many objections which may be urged against my theory" - Charles Darwin.

On the Origin of Species was published in the year 1859, and actually focuses more on the connection among species and all things from a single source, rather than the "survival of the fittest" theories taught in schools and reported in mainstream biology and science publications, where Darwin's theory of evolution appears to be in direct conflict with all traditional theories of human origin through divine intervention, and is used as a tool to further separate science and spirituality, regardless of his advice.

Today a large body of evidence affirms that his findings do not fully explain human origin or prove that we are part of the same evolutionary process as plants and other animals; however, we are still shown images of our ape-like "ancestors" in current biology books and publications. We even have names for the first man and woman, George and Lucy, which concludes that we are a part of their family tree; although, there is no incontrovertible evidence of a transitional species, such as homo neanderthalensis.

A study published in Proceedings of the National Academy of Sciences in the year 2003 compared DNA from our earliest confirmed ancestors with neanderthal DNA and stated, "Our results add to the evidence collected previously in different fields, making the hypothesis of a neanderthal heritage very unlikely". Terms and acronyms, such as early modern human (EMH) and anatomically modern human (AMH), replaced the previous descriptor, Cro-Magnon, as unbiased, modern scientists now realize that the hairy cavemen portrayed in movies and cartoons are not necessarily our ancestors.

In fact, our genetic code and appearance remain unchanged for at least 250,000 years, which is as far back as they can date EMHs. Our actual ancestors might not have behaved like us, but they definitely looked like us.

So, we are not evolutionary descendants of homo neanderthalensis, but some carry trace amounts of their DNA. It is theorized that homo sapiens almost became extinct at the hands of the larger and stronger neanderthals, who ate the men and mated with the women until the population was reduced to approximately fifty homo sapiens. The survivors retreated to caves and began the ongoing process of constructing massive underground dwellings.

Perhaps they were not exposed to an event that forced the neanderthals to extinction or found a way to resurface and exterminate them. Repopulating from roughly fifty people seems to explain the extreme lack of diversity in the DNA of modern humans. We are almost genetically identical to each other in comparison to the diversity of all other known species.

After searching for 150 years, mainstream science claims to have found the missing link in the year 2009, proposing that the fossils of Australopithecus Sediba closely link us to apes. We have an inherent need for resolution and the habit of settling for preconceived conclusions that fit into a neat little box, where there is rarely room for the whole truth. Human history is littered with theories that attempt to separate us from spirituality, and it often seems comforting to accept them rather than remain undecided.

The process of living cells randomly mutating (evolving) over long periods of time does not even begin to explain the complexities of human beings, and a growing body of evidence points to an undeniable intervention of intelligent design. We are evolving, along with the rest of the Cosmos, but not in the way we were taught to think of evolution. We are becoming more complex beings, with increasing levels of consciousness, as the frequency of the Earth and our entire Universe increases.

The Hundredth Monkey Effect

In the year 1987 DNA researchers from the Universities of California and Michigan announced that all humans descended from a single Mitochondrial Eve, the MRCA (most recent common ancestor) in a direct maternal line. Her mate was confirmed a few years later and they lived in Africa between 250,000 and 270,000 years ago. Being in our existing form for that long means that we have gone through the Cycle of Ages at least ten times and explains how so much more was commonly known about how the Universe works before science became grounded in and limited to the physical world. We could loosely equate Newton's mechanical universe discoveries to the guy that "invented" halitosis by blowing into his hand. They are accurate physical observations, with no explanation of the underlying creative forces.

We can begin to solve the mystery of our existence and realize the power that comes with that knowledge after we detach from the preconceived limitations forced on us by mainstream science. Today we are working below the nanoscopic level (one billionth of a meter) and continue to explore the macroscopic. We have rediscovered the true meaning of the phrase, "As above, so below", and have the growing ability to scientifically affirm metaphysical knowledge. The accurate modern (and ancient) concept of the word, *spirituality*, is *the scientific observation of Nature*. But before we address the mechanics of existence, we will explore a fascinating example of evolution and innate knowledge:

The Macaca Fuscata Japanese monkey had been observed in the wild for more than thirty years. Scientists began dropping raw sweet potatoes in the sand on the island of Koshima in the year 1952. The monkeys loved them but did not like the dirt and sand. An eighteen-month-old female discovered that she could remove it by washing the sweet potatoes in a nearby stream. She taught her mother and playmates, who taught their mothers and the other children. By the year 1958 all the young monkeys on the island were washing their sweet potatoes, but only the adults that imitated their children made that social improvement. The others kept eating dirty potatoes.

Then something amazing was observed. One morning almost every monkey on Koshima Island began washing their sweet potatoes in the stream, without any individual instruction. Then colonies of monkeys on the other islands and the mainland tribe at Takasakiyama began to do the same. The scientists determined that once a critical percentage of monkeys learned this new trait, the rest of them instinctively learned, without being taught or imitating the other monkeys. The explanation was first introduced by biologist Lyall Watson and Ken Keyes provided this colorful description:

"Let us suppose that when the sun rose one morning there were ninety-nine monkeys on Koshima Island who had learned to wash their sweet potatoes. Let's further suppose that later that morning the hundredth monkey learned to wash potatoes. Then it happened! By that evening almost everyone in the tribe was washing sweet potatoes before eating them. The added energy of this hundredth monkey somehow created an ideological breakthrough! Thus, when a certain critical number achieves an awareness, this new awareness may be communicated from mind to mind.

Although the exact number may vary, this Hundredth Monkey Phenomenon means that when only a limited number of people know of a new way, it may remain the conscious property of these people. But there is a point at which if only one more person tunes in to a new awareness, a field is strengthened so that this awareness is picked up by almost everyone!"

The Akasha

The transference of ideas among species works the same way for all sentient beings. We are all immersed in a Unified Field of Information, also known as the Global Mind, or what modern science termed the Universal Bank of Knowledge, anciently known as the *Akasha*, a Sanskrit term for the element, ether, in traditional Indian cosmology and the direct Hindu translation is *sky*. Many scientists now believe, as the ancients knew, that even our memories are stored there in lieu of the brain, which acts as an antenna for the heart, which transmits and receives information to and from our DNA, which structures, maintains or changes our physical existence based on the exchange of information.

In fact, the heart's electrical field is one hundred times stronger than the brain's and its magnetic field is five thousand times stronger. Brain tissue and heart tissue are basically the same, as our bodies and all things are comprised of the same stuff: carbon, hydrogen, oxygen, and nitrogen. Cells are cells and it has become evident that each one has an individual consciousness, as well as being interconnected, just like us. We are cells of the Earth, just as our individual cells are the cells of our bodies.

I had just begun to study the human chakra system and learned that the main location is at the heart, which did not make sense, I thought it was just an involuntary pump, but that is only its physical function. Soon after that I saw an experiment performed by the Heart Math Institute, which confirmed that the heart deciphers information before the brain:

Participants, fitted with head and chest electrodes, were shown various, random images on computer screens. The heart reacted first, but not from the physical images. It had a positive or negative reaction two seconds before the images were selected and shown, which substantiates the heart's significance and affirms the existence of the Unified Field.

Anyone can easily witness this field of information and communication by observing birds and fish move in perfect unison, or accomplished dancers and athletes perform at high speeds. We see no delays within the flock's or school's directional changes, and we can move our body parts in very complicated synchronicity faster than the electrical signals in our bodies can travel to and from our brains. Traditional physics does not and cannot explain those phenomena, while ancient philosophy does.

The Akasha has recorded and is transmitting every event and thought transmission since the beginning of existence, and we are always exchanging information with others at the same level of consciousness. Our thought waves behave like radio and other waves of information. We cannot see them because they are outside of the visible light section of the electromagnetic spectrum, along with all things of different *dimensions* (levels of vibration) we cannot sense. However, we can tune our minds to this invisible bank of mental energy, just as we can tune a radio to an invisible but tangible signal.

There are many benefits to tuning in, some you will soon discover and more will follow, but there are issues that result from errant thought transmissions to and from the Unified Field. One being it makes it too easy and comfortable to attach to a specific set of beliefs, and when enough people are misled, many others at the same consciousness level automatically adopt their false beliefs. Fortunately, when enough people discover and accept the truth, many more will instantly become aware. Imagine what would happen if we increased our awareness, expanded our consciousness and learned to rise above low thought transmissions to access the divinity within the Akasha.

Good Vibrations

And that is exactly what is taking place today. A prophesied shift in global consciousness is well underway and evidenced by an increase in the Earth's vibrational *frequency* (pulse, cycles per second, *hertz*).

The Earth's atmosphere carries an electrical charge, current and voltage, which would quickly diffuse without a source. At any given moment there are approximately a thousand lightning storms occurring simultaneously, and the atmosphere acts as a weak conductor. There is an electromagnetic "cavity" between the surface of the Earth and the inner edge of the ionosphere, about thirty-three miles above the surface, and there is a vertical current flow within this cavity that produces a charge of quasi-standing electromagnetic waves, which were first detected and measured by German physicist, W.O. Schumann in the year 1954.

These waves occur at specific frequencies of 7.8, 14, 20, 26, and 45 hertz. Many scientists believe that the base frequency of what became known as the Schumann Resonance remained at 7.8 hertz for thousands of years, until the year 1980, when it began to rise dramatically. Some people, including myself, believe that time seems to go by faster and the days feel shorter as the frequency rises, but that could just be an effect of aging, or maybe awareness.

We share this pulse with the Earth and the rest of the Universe, and our level of consciousness is increasing along with our vibrational frequency. Our DNA is currently being upgraded, and many are becoming more intuitive and instinctively moving away from materialism and external technologies, and back to Nature and internal technologies, just as the Mayans predicted.

In the year 1967 Swiss doctor, Hans Jenny, published his first volume of Cymatics: The Study of Wave Phenomena, which provided written and photographic documentation of the effects of sound vibrations on fluids, powders and liquid pastes. He found that simple and basic patterns were formed when a slow vibration passed through a form of media, and the patterns became more complex as the frequency increased.

In fact, the higher frequencies created many of the same archetypal patterns previously documented by ancient Sumerians and Egyptians and are a part of their Sacred Geometry. Modern science continues to affirm what the ancients knew; vibration is the foundation of all existence.

"There is no spoon" - The Matrix

Now let's get back to that dream, the seemingly long one, which we all share. When most of us think about physics, we think of math, but here our system of numbers can only be an attempt to measure the immeasurable and quantify that which cannot be quantified. There actually is no such thing as "one" because an infinite number of things comprise one, and one is a part of an infinite number of things.

"As a physicist, that is, a man who had devoted his whole life to wholly prosaic science, the exploration of matter, no one would surely suspect me of being a fantast. And so, having studied the atom, I am telling you that there is no matter as such! All matter arises and persists only due to a force that causes the atomic particles to vibrate, holding them together in the tiniest of solar systems, the atom. Yet in the whole of the Universe, there is no force that is either intelligent or eternal, and we must therefore assume that behind this force there is a conscious, intelligent mind or spirit. This is the very origin of all matter" - Max Planck (1858-1947), 1918 Nobel Prize winner and Quantum Theory founder.

Noticing the similar behaviors of atoms and solar systems was the first realization I had on my own when I began to study *Quantum Mechanics*, but I would have grasped the concept much sooner had I thought more about the simple definition, *the measurement of energy*. My mind quickly compared that to existing information, and I briefly related it to a unit of measure, like an amp in electricity, but that is *a* measurement of energy. *The* measurement of energy, the act of measuring, is the creative force.

Our physically grounded belief system tells us that we are merely passive *observers*, pawns of fate on a rock flying through space without any control over our surroundings; however, the truth is we live in a *Participatory* Universe, which we create with the act of *measuring* (seeing, hearing, smelling, tasting, and feeling). The act of observing and the act of creating are one in the same and we are co-creators.

"In our search to find the smallest particle of matter and our quest to define the edge of the Universe, this relationship suggests that we may never find either. No matter how deeply we peer into the quantum world of the atom or how far we reach into the vastness of outer space, the act of us looking with the expectation that something exists may be precisely the force that creates something for us to see" - Gregg Braden (scientist, spiritualist; integrator).

When we look at an atom, it appears to be more than ninety-five percent empty space, and if we take any particle of that atom and magnify it, we find more atoms with mostly empty space. Magnify a particle from one of those atoms and we find, you guessed it, more atoms and more space. It is infinite at the microscopic level and also infinite at the macroscopic, with solar systems, galaxies and possibly universes all behaving identically, with roughly the same ratio of what appears to be empty space.

A picture of an atom would reflect a nucleus of protons and neutrons surrounded by a certain number of orbiting electrons. A moment later a second picture would reflect more or less orbiting electrons. They seem to vanish and reappear in different locations when they vibrate too fast or slow.

If we study the electromagnetic spectrum of light, we notice that the visible section is very small, which explains the illusion of empty space. Anything vibrating too fast for us to sense is known as ultraviolet (above violet) and includes x-rays and gamma rays. Anything vibrating too slow for us to sense is known as infrared (below red) and includes micro waves and radio waves.

In the year 1801 Thomas Young performed and documented the first double slit experiment, in which a beam of light was directed through a plate with two slits, and onto an observation screen. The *wave* of light passed through both slits, and an interference pattern was created on the screen. In a later experiment, a single photon (*particle* of light) was used. Unexpectedly, an interference pattern was created on the screen, and it appeared that the particle became a wave and passed through both slits, so an electron detector was placed before the plate and revealed that it was only passing through one.

Then the electron detector was placed after the plate and the single photon appeared on the screen, apparently remaining a particle, and clumping patterns were created when directing multiple photons onto the screen, nothing like the interference pattern made with waves. It was determined that the act of observing waves is what causes them to collapse into particles.

The scientists realized and concluded that their presence, thoughts and expectations were affecting the outcomes, and their double slit experiments revealed the basis of what is known as the particle/wave duality, in which all particles are actually parts of electromagnetic waves and only become isolated particles when we measure (observe) them.

There is no such thing as empty space and anything that exists anywhere as a particle exists everywhere as a wave. We turn waves into particles (matter) by observing them and bringing them to a level of vibration (dimension) we can sense. That is how all things are connected and in the year 1997 it was physically proven. Dr. Nicolas Gisin and colleagues from the University of Geneva sent pairs of photons in opposite directions along optical fibers, like those used for phone lines. When they were at the ends of the lines, over seven miles apart, a stimulus was applied to one of the photons and the other responded instantaneously. There was no delay, and it was determined that distance was not a factor. They could have been at opposite ends of the Universe and still would have reacted simultaneously.

The information from the stimulus was not traveling faster than we can measure or faster than the speed of light, it was not traveling at all. The photons were never separated because they were two particles of the same wave, which exists everywhere at the same time in the higher dimensions.

Those facts lend understanding to Einstein's realization that space and time are relative and cannot be separated. Time gives legitimacy to matter and does not exist in the higher dimensions. It is something we experience by putting things in motion and creating cycles. That is why an astronaut's rate of aging decreases when they are moving through space, and how our ancestors were able to view the future by studying the Cosmos over long periods of time. Today, by studying the microscopic world over short periods of time, we can affirm their knowledge of how larger things function.

I trust that you will not limit the quantum world to the subatomic, and please do not shy away from any revelations as you begin to accept and further explore this empowering information. Sooner or later the power of thought and intent will become evident, and you will realize that the entire construct of space/time/matter is the Grand Illusion. “A wise man, recognizing that the world is but an illusion, does not act if it is real, so he escapes the suffering” - the Buddha.

A Holographic Universe

Everything in our Universe, including us, is comprised of atoms. We are particles of electromagnetic waves and exist everywhere in what is known as the *Non-local Consciousness*, also known as the One Mind, the Single Source, the Singularity, or God. The *Local Consciousness* is our individual mind, or Ego Mind. The most direct religious reference to that understanding I have found is the Buddhist concept of Multiplicity, in which we consist of numerous individual minds, gathering knowledge and gaining experience for the One Mind, to which we are directly connected.

This is only a personal realization, just a thought I had about the Big Bang Theory when I began integrating science and spirituality, but perhaps it will shed some light on the concept of our perceived physical existence: Imagine you are without form and floating in a sea of nothingness. You cannot see, hear, smell, taste, feel, or experience time, but you can think, therefore you *are*, you exist. That seems boring and frustrating, so what would you do?

Maybe you would try to achieve a "physical" existence, create and evolve a world over time and assume multiple forms to obtain multiple perspectives. That is what I would do and perhaps that's what we did. Our Universe appears to be expanding because our consciousness is expanding, and consciousness is what manifests all things into physical existence.

"In Quantum Physics, objects are not determined things of Newtonian vintage. Instead, they are waves of possibility. When we observe, these waves "collapse" into actual events in our experience. Instead of spread-out waves what we observe is a localized particle. This is the famous observer effect. In this generalized science within consciousness, upward causation gives us the waves of possibility to choose from; downward causation consists of the act of choice" - Amit Goswami, PhD.

Within these waves, unlimited possibilities exist for everything that manifests into our reality. The probability that requires the least amount of energy will manifest, unless we focus our energy on another possible reality. That does not mean that we can individually and instantly alter everyone's reality. It is our united consciousness that chooses actuality from multiple quantum possibilities; however, we can choose to alter our individual perception of reality, which has a profound effect on the whole because we are consciousness conductors, and our Universe is holographic in nature.

Holography is defined as *a technique for recording, then reconstructing, the amplitude and phase distributions of a coherent wave disturbance used to produce three-dimensional images (holograms)*. By definition, we tend to limit that to our sense of sight, but when we include all three-dimensional senses, we can begin to understand that our world is a *projection* of our collective thought and intent.

When you change anything within a hologram, that change is reflected throughout the whole and when enough people project the same change, it manifests into reality. So, your perception (recording) of the world constructs your individual reality, and your projection of that perception to the hologram can eventually alter (reconstruct) everyone's reality.

Consciousness

To affirm that our thoughts impact our surroundings, and all things have consciousness, let's consider another experiment performed by the Heart Math Institute: A cup of yogurt was placed in front of a participant. The yogurt had electrodes attached to a device that measures frequency, but the participant did not have any electrodes attached to the device or the yogurt. The controller made statements that made the person happy, and the yogurt's level of vibration increased. When the person was made sad or angry, the yogurt's level of vibration decreased.

We positively or negatively affect everything and everyone, especially those within our local circle of energy, which extends about six to eight feet from our physical bodies. And what is your physical body? It is a liquid crystal. Your body is the most organized form of matter in a mostly liquid form, with the highest potential level of consciousness.

Obviously, there are many different levels. A quartz crystal has a higher level than a brick, but the brick still has consciousness because it exists. Plants have a higher level than most of us realize. They respond accordingly to positive and negative emotions and have incredible adaptation abilities.

A fly's level is so low, in comparison to ours, that when one is swatted and killed, it does not realize it has left its physical body, it just keeps flying along in its ethereal body until it assumes another physical form. Most animals only feel love or fear and are free from the distractions and attachments that come with complex emotions (feelings). That is how they are so in tune with their surroundings and acutely aware of the frequency and intent of other animals and people. Birds in the condor family, such as jays, crows and parakeets, have a very high level of awareness and the amazing ability to use tools and solve problems. Elephants are actually very smart and so are apes and many other species, but the most intelligent known species are dolphins, which theoretically utilize more of their brains than humans.

Some believe that horses, dogs, cats, and other domesticated animals experience complex emotions as we do, perhaps due to their long relationships with human beings, but they definitely have not lost the abilities that extend beyond their physical senses as we have. All animals are acutely aware of their true surroundings, and they instinctively react and interact with other creatures and people by perceiving their projection of love or fear.

Love, Fear & DNA

There are only two emotions: Love and Fear. All derivatives are classified as *complex emotions* or *feelings*, and hate is actually a form of fear. Simply thinking in terms of the two base emotions and releasing all attachment to past experiences allows us to have a clear perspective and we can begin to better control our complex emotions, while fully experiencing them and allowing them to serve their purpose. We are always experiencing and projecting either love or fear, regardless of how complicated our feelings become. Love is the high and fast frequency. Fear is the low and slow.

Within our DNA, there are sixty-four potential coding sites where information can be exchanged. Currently only twenty of them are active (these are our twenty amino acids). That alone fascinates and sparks a barrage of questions... Why are only twenty active, and have more than twenty ever been active? Who or what might be turning them on and off, and is it possible for us to turn them on and off?

The answer to the last question is yes, we control the function of the active coding sites and have the growing ability to activate the others and upgrade our DNA. We might think of it as flipping the switches that raise our frequency. Scientists believe that the current, average human consciousness level is around three out of a possible ten, which is the same ratio as the active to inactive coding sites. So, what is the key to proper functioning of the active coding sites and activation of the others? Love!

The short and fast wavelength of love comes into contact with much more of our DNA than the long and slow wavelength of fear. Vibrating in the high frequency of love expands our DNA and vibrating in the low frequency of fear literally shrinks it, even when it has been removed from the body.

The military performed a series of experiments in the 1990s, in which leukocytes (white blood cells) were collected from donors and DNA samples were placed into chambers where they could measure electrical changes. The donors were placed in rooms fifty miles away and subjected to emotional stimulation. Their separated DNA reacted accordingly and instantaneously.

The Heart Math Institute published a study titled Local and Non-Local Effects of Coherent Heart Frequencies on Conformational Changes of DNA. Human placenta DNA (the most pristine form) was placed in twenty-eight vials and given to twenty-eight researchers, each trained to generate and feel strong emotions. The DNA changed shape according to the feelings of the researchers. When they felt love, happiness and gratitude, the strands unwound, and the DNA expanded. When they felt fear, anger and frustration, the DNA contracted and turned off some of the active coding sites.

Long-term studies completed over the last two decades suggest that we are not condemned by our genes. Potential negative issues decrease to or below average levels when children are removed from the source and belief that they are doomed to suffer the diseases and conditions in their family history. Furthermore, children removed early can look more like their adopted parents as adults. Our genome is not set in stone as previously believed. It is not a complete "blueprint" and only contains instructions for basic formations. Many of the details are governed by environment, habits and beliefs.

The Hado Effect

Dr. Masaru Emoto, chief researcher at the Hado Institute in Tokyo, Japan, performed and documented numerous experiments that demonstrate the impact of our emotions on water. He released a book in the year 1999 titled The Message from Water, which became so popular that the phenomenon became known as the *Hado* Effect, and he defined hado as *the intrinsic vibration pattern at the atomic level in all matter, the smallest unit of energy. Its basis is the energy of human consciousness.*

He gathered polluted and clean water from multiple locations and studied the crystallization process during and after freezing. The heavily polluted samples did not form any crystals, while clean mineral spring water formed beautiful ice crystals. That was expected, but there were inconsistencies among identical samples, and the only possible variable was his mood, so he used identical tap water samples and projected negative emotions onto some, and positive onto the others before freezing. The negative samples did not crystallize, and the positive samples formed beautiful and organized crystals.

Then he began to attach positive and negative words to the samples and had people bless and curse samples, all resulting in the same fashion. On July 25th, 1999, he led 350 people in blessing heavily polluted Lake Biwa, making a dramatic improvement in water quality and greatly reducing the algae and foul smell. "Since all phenomena are at heart resonating energy, by changing the vibration we can change the substance" - Dr. Masaru Emoto. The human body is more than seventy percent liquid, so if our thoughts have a dramatic effect on water, and they do, just imagine the impact they have on us.

Two Seconds To Peace

This is not science fiction or myth. Our innate ability to experience and project the high frequency of love to help others and improve our surroundings is an internal technology that we can practice and eventually master. I love acronyms, they are a great way to help me remember, so I placed two sticky notes on my kitchen cabinet when I began to focus on vibrating at a higher frequency. One read TNL (that's not love), which helped me to catch myself and refocus if I became and remained negative.

The other read BLT (bless, love and thank), which reminded me not to judge, but rather to bless every situation and be thankful for everything, which is especially beneficial in the kitchen, where our mood definitely affects our food and drink. Gratitude is the strongest positive complex emotion, and we can raise any vibration by being truly thankful. Blessing what we consume (and all things) reduces toxins and helps our bodies deal with unhealthy choices, especially the ones we know are unhealthy.

Thanking a higher power, such as the Source or the Universe, is very effective; however, asking an external being to bless something for us is not nearly as effective as blessing it ourselves. We are on top of the situation and know what is needed. Why ask for outside help when we can do it? Some believe that they are not holy and have no power to bless anything, and that delusion is the only preventative factor. Accept that you are a god in the making, a co-creator with limitless potential and power, and you only need to realize and have faith in your abilities to develop and utilize them.

I initially understood the concept of Two Seconds to Peace to be an exaggeration, but it is a true guideline and a reachable goal. Eventually we can experience and control negative emotions, without any lingering attachments, and quickly return to a high frequency. We still feel deeply and sincerely but instinctively know that negative vibrations are harmful, and the best remedies are always peace and balance. It will start with better reactions to small inconveniences, like spilling coffee or taking a wrong turn, then larger issues will cease to control your thoughts when you are not resolving them, for which you become better prepared. Ultimately even the adverse emotional effects of tragic news will be instantly minimized.

Gnothe Seauton

"You have tremendous capacities, far more and far greater than you suspect. You have been taught, or you have taught yourself, certain skills of hand or mind in order that you may contribute the fruits of these skills to the general economy and thus earn a livelihood. This is normal practice. Yet if you had been encouraged to spend the same time and effort in learning about yourself and proper instruction had been available to you, your contribution to the general good would be fifty times greater than it is and the rewards to you proportionate. Since it is never too late to learn, start now to study yourself" - Joseph Weed. "He who knows others is wise. He who knows himself is enlightened" - Lao Tzu.

The great philosophers during the Golden Age of Greece inscribed the words, *Gnothe Seauton*, over the entrance of the Athenian Temple. They mean *Know Thyself*, which is the essential requirement to all knowledge and wisdom. The fact that we have a record of our experiences often leads us to believe that we already know ourselves well; however, if we cannot transform that information into knowledge and wisdom, there is obviously much more to learn. One way to better know ourselves is to apply critical thought to past and current experiences.

Most of the time when we believe we are thinking, we are only recreating old emotional occurrences, while what is needed is to discover their purpose and relevance. Understanding that every thought and event happen for a reason, the most important question is *why*. We must dig deeper to make sense of our thoughts and feelings, which is paramount to controlling and utilizing our emotions to help manifest our desired reality.

The Feeling Is The Prayer

Let's go much deeper and elaborate on this statement from earlier in the chapter: The brain acts as an antenna for the heart, which transmits and receives information to and from our DNA, which structures, maintains or changes our physical existence based on the exchange of information. What information are we sending to our bodies and other entities, and what information are we sending to the Source?

Those that pray normally do so in one of four modes: An *informal* prayer is thanking or asking for something appropriate at the time. A *petition* prayer is a request made for things desired. A *ritualistic* prayer is an obligation of faith to be performed at specific times and/or places, and *meditative* prayer is concentrating on requests, gratitude and Divine knowledge or beings for longer periods. All can be beneficial, as positive intent and gratitude raise our vibrations, but there is a lesser-known and more beneficial fifth mode of prayer, where we *feel* the feeling that the prayer has already been answered.

All traditional modes of prayer are basically requests and by asking for something we acknowledge that it is not occurring. That is the message the heart transmits to the Source and Akasha, so that's the information the Source returns to structure the body and eventual reality. For example, “Let there be peace on Earth” means there is no peace, which creates a cycle that cannot be broken until enough of us believe or learn to feel that there is peace. We must focus on the desired outcome as if it already exists.

The teachings in the unedited Bible advise us to, “Ask without hidden motive and be surrounded by your answer, be enveloped by what you desire that your gladness be full”. In his book titled The Power of Awareness, Neville Goddard wrote, “You must make your future dream a present fact by assuming the feeling of your wish fulfilled until your assumption has all the sensory vividness of reality”.

What is the first thing parents and others that take care of children say and feel when a child is injured? “You're fine, you're okay, you're alright.” We instinctively do that in strenuous situations, and we can get into the habit of doing it consciously and often. If we want peace, we say and feel, “There *is* peace”. If we want someone to be healed, we say and feel, “You *are* healed”.

In the fifth mode of prayer, the observer is a confident creator, and words only reinforce the feeling; however, not every feeling is a prayer. We must unite raw emotion and focused thought to achieve the desired feeling. The base emotion of love is formed in the lower chakras and thought, free of judgment and ego (hidden motive), is formed in the higher chakras. They are combined to create the feeling and transmitted to the Source and intended recipients by the center chakra at the heart. That can be done informally, for what is appropriate at the time, and meditatively for longer periods of time and specific results, which can occur quickly or gradually. Keep in mind that thought without judgment includes all attachment to outcome, meaning we must accept that other factors might prevent or alter the intended reality.

If multiple quantum possibilities (waves) are occurring for every actual reality, and they are, giving our energy to a particular outcome (particle) surely increases its chances of becoming reality. To affect atoms (matter), we must change the energy the atom is in by communicating in a way it understands. The Unified Field recognizes the feeling from the heart when we project our thoughts and emotions.

Five Tenets To Compassion

Compassion is thought without attachment, feeling without distortion and emotion without charge. *Thought without attachment* means that we do not judge situations, occurrences, others, or ourselves, and we consciously honor and respect all experiences and relationships. *Feeling without distortion* is experiencing complex emotions without the interference of previous negative experiences, as releasing attachments to past pains allows us to obtain and maintain a clear perspective. *Emotion without charge* is feeling without creating and holding an emotional charge that will eventually be a past pain.

The Essenes were an enlightened fellowship of men and women that inhabited the areas of Qumran, Ein Gedi and Jerusalem around two thousand years ago. Their existence and the extent of their wisdom was confirmed with the discovery of the Dead Sea Scrolls in the year 1947. They advised us to embrace all negative experiences, as negative emotions are indicators of what we are to examine- not suppress. In fact, experiencing emotions is one of our reasons for being here. They are physical phenomena, and like time, do not exist in the higher dimensions. This is not to say that we should condone or comply with the unfair, but we must accept and bless all circumstances beyond our control, rather than worry about them, which strengthens the negative conditions we fear and decreases the likelihood of change.

In addition to their insightful definitions, they gave us five tenets to truly experience compassion: First, *acknowledge* that there is a single source of existence. Second, *trust* the process of life as it is. Third, *believe* that every experience is an opportunity to demonstrate mastery- not a test to pass or fail. Fourth, *believe* that your life mirrors your quest to know yourself in all ways by finding your extremes to achieve balance. Fifth, *believe* that your life essence is eternal, and your body may also experience it. Any of the five tenets not acknowledged, trusted or believed defines the next step to mastery.

Seven Mirrors Of Self

When we find fault in others, when we judge them, we are actually judging ourselves. There is some issue within us that we are denying and directly or indirectly imposing on them. Realizing the deeper purpose of what is taking place is the first step in these situations. Then we can determine and address our internal issues, which can be very similar or completely different from the faults we find in others.

The Essenes taught that each moment of our lives the reality of what we have become is mirrored to us by the actions, choices and language of those around us, and there are seven mirrors we use to view and know ourselves. Some are fairly obvious, and some are subtle and require more thought.

First and most obvious is the mirror of *the moment*, in which our presence and what we are projecting is directly reflected by those around us at that particular moment. Second is the mirror of *that which is judged*, where the faults we find in those around us are indicators of our internal issues. When someone repeatedly shows us the same negative patterns, those two mirrors most likely reflect our internal truth. Third is the mirror of *that which is lost, given or taken away*. We feel a strong connection when in the presence of someone who possesses a quality or perspective we had and lost at some point in our lives. We should determine what they have that we lost, gave away or had taken away, and the relevance.

Fourth and more subtle is the mirror of *most forgotten love*. Here we are able to see ourselves in the presence of addictive or compulsive habits and relationships, where we gradually give away the things that are most important to us and have the opportunity to view ourselves as we lose what we hold dear. Fifth is the mirror of *father and mother*, in which the actions of our parents toward us reflect our own beliefs and expectations and allow the most insight into the choices we make throughout our lives. For example, if we constantly feel judged, or that our best is never good enough, it is likely that what is being mirrored is our own belief that we are not good enough and are not behaving as we should.

Sixth is the mirror of *your quest into darkness*. In this mirror, we see ourselves without the thoughts and constructs we build to keep us safe and learn to trust the process of life as it is. The "dark knight of the soul" subconsciously leads us to extremes in order to find the balance between them, and within ourselves. The most difficult situations provide the best opportunities to demonstrate mastery of our emotions, balance our karma and know ourselves in all ways. Fortunately, we will not be faced with such necessary challenges until we have acquired the tools to overcome them.

Seventh and most subtle is the mirror of *self-perception*. This teaches us to allow for the possibility that all life experiences and every aspect of our lives are perfect in nature and the only thing preventing that belief is the act of comparison. Experience, accomplishments, financial status, physical condition, and all other individual aspects can only be judged by using an external reference, which removes us from the truth that all circumstances are serving specific purposes and perfection is only a perception.

Going deeper we find there are Three Universal Fears that we manifest in our relationships in order to overcome them, and they will continue to occur until we master the situations and resulting emotions. First is the fear of *abandonment and separation*, a strong, instinctive feeling enhanced by past pains. Second is the fear of *unworthiness and inadequacy*, that we are not or never will be good enough, and Third is the fear of *trust and surrender*, which includes trusting others, ourselves and the process of life.

The Four Noble Truths

The typical association we have with the word, surrender, is giving up or quitting. Similar is the association with a white flag, which is symbolic of peace- not surrender. That is by design and all mainstream teachings and surface meanings in religion tell us to give all our power to an external source or being, to surrender ourselves to statutory law and God's will. An example is the AA twelve-step process, which is successful and encouraging due to the intent, fellowship and assistance, but would be much more beneficial if it utilized our internal power instead of giving it away and asking for help.

Muhammad's explanation of surrender is closely aligned with the Buddhist philosophy of radical acceptance and the relative, deeper messages in the Bible. The difference in the average conception and true meaning appear non-existent or very subtle to most people that receive this information and only become apparent to a small minority.

The Buddha realized that and actually became frustrated to the point that he considered not teaching the masses, but he continued and began calling his doctrine the Secret Oral Teachings. "I have discovered a profound truth, difficult to perceive, difficult to understand, accessible only to the wise. Of what use to reveal to men that which I have discovered at the price of laborious efforts. This doctrine cannot be understood by those filled with desire and hatred; it is mysterious, deep and hidden from the vulgar mind. These teachings are not called secret because it is forbidden to talk about them, they are secret because so few who hear them understand."

The Buddha (enlightened one) was a prince born in the area of Lumbini, Nepal about 2,500 years ago and named Siddhartha Gautama. A sage predicted that he would become a great king or a great spiritual leader, so the king tried to isolate him from experiences that might have put him on the spiritual path. He lived in the luxury of their palace and did not leave the grounds until the age of twenty-nine. Shocked by the suffering of all living beings, he was compelled to leave his family and riches behind to experience suffering and find a way to end it. He mastered many forms of yoga and meditation and experienced his extremes until he developed all positive qualities and eliminated all negative qualities, achieving total awareness under a bodhi tree in Bodhgaya, India at the age of thirty-five. Seven weeks later he began teaching the Noble Truths as the inevitable path to Nirvana:

1 - Life Means Suffering	2 - The Cause Is Attachment
3 - Suffering Can End	4 - The Noble Path

First are the three types: *Suffering of Suffering* is physical pain, illness and discomfort. *Suffering of Change* is our obvious fear of aging and death, but less examined is the fear that the positive things in our lives will change or be lost, causing suffering even for those who have fulfilled all of their desires. *All-pervasive Suffering* means that all human beings inevitably suffer in overcoming the obstacles necessary to find balance and experience peace, happiness, compassion, enlightenment, and ascension.

Second are the three causes: *Attachment* is the tension and stress created by the underlying awareness that everything which has a beginning will have an ending. *Anger* is a negative projection that causes harm to others and you, and *Ignorance* is the result of ignoring reality and the Ultimate Truth.

Third is that suffering can end. The causes of suffering are completely dependent on our state of mind and by changing our minds we can eventually break the cycles and enter *Nirvana* (the state beyond all suffering). We can overcome all delusions of reality and end suffering with the proper practices.

Fourth are the correct attitudes and actions of the Eight-fold Noble Path: Correct *Thought* is realizing the impact our thoughts have on others, ourselves and the Hologram. Correct *Speech* is being honest, avoiding gossip and the use of negative words and harsh tones. Correct *Action* is utilizing proper thought to translate knowledge into wisdom and avoid causing harm.

Correct *Livelihood* is providing for yourself and dependents using correct thought, speech and action. Correct *Understanding* is applying critical thought to test information and translate it into knowledge. Correct *Effort* is joyful perseverance and overcoming plateaus and declines in progress along the path. Correct *Mindfulness* is learning from the past, planning for the future, but living in the present. Correct *Concentration* is developing and maintaining a calm, attentive and balanced state of mind.

The Buddha said there are Four Yardsticks we can use to measure our progress along the Noble Path. Love, compassion, happiness, and joyous effort will be experienced when we are practicing correctly. In his and other Eastern philosophies, surrender is not quitting or giving up your freedom and power, it is ridding yourself of all delusions, accepting reality, redefining freedom, and developing your power.

Karma

Karma is a Hindu word meaning action, which was changed to the results of action; however, not all circumstances are the result of karma. Occurrences that do not originate with conscious intent are classified as *causality* (the law of cause and effect). Therefore, *karma* is truly defined as *the process of cause and effect resulting from the thoughts and decisions of conscious beings capable of free choice.*

An acorn falling from a branch and making a splash in a pond is an example of causality, while a squirrel dropping an acorn from the branch and making a splash because he tried to carry too many is an example of instant karma. The acorns will have a similar effect on the pond and surroundings, but the squirrel was impacted by its own decision. If you throw a pebble in a pond, you create a ripple that perpetuates in all directions and comes back to you. Now apply that metaphorically, with your thoughts and actions as the pebble and the impact ripples across the holographic pond and back to you.

When spiritual masters teach about loving your enemies, that is for your benefit as much as theirs. All negative thoughts and actions impact others and come back to us as negative karma, while positive projections create positive results. If we feel unhappy or unsuccessful, we are experiencing the results of previous negative thoughts and actions, and that will continue until we balance our karma with positive thoughts and actions, which can take years, decades and even lifetimes. We can also have an imbalance of too much positive karma, which must be corrected to achieve balance and ascension.

Groups of individual conscious minds form entities that create group karma, which will require balance within itself and with other groups. An obvious example within the permanent group of a family with two siblings is when one child misbehaves and is reprimanded, the other sprouts wings and is praised. More subtle occurrences can be observed by accepting the fact that karma is always at work, and we eventually realize that all perceived external enemies are only the ego mind's projections of enemies.

Thoughts Are Things

The Chandra Observatory, launched from the Space Shuttle Columbia in the year 1999, utilizes x-ray telescopes to produce fascinating images and has confirmed that filaments of energy are present throughout the ninety-five percent of the observable Universe that appears to us as empty space. These ultraviolet filaments are very similar to brain neurons in appearance and provide further confirmation that all things are connected. What else might we find beyond the visible section of light and our perceivable dimensions?

There are four energy bodies within and around our physical bodies that exist in the finer grades of matter of the higher dimensions, and the higher the vibrational frequency, the finer the matter and body. From lowest to highest, they are the *ethereal* body, the *emotional* or *astral* body, the *mental* body, and the *spiritual* body. It is possible for a trained consciousness to travel outside of the physical body on the mental and astral planes, and emotional/astral travel is more difficult as the mental plane is less dense.

Surrounding and influencing those bodies are the energy bodies created by our thoughts and will. When we have a thought, an entity is created and repeating that thought strengthens the connection and creates a permanent "being". These beings collectively and physically manifest through our senses and translate everything we experience. At the same time the corresponding synapse (connection point) in the brain is strengthened and becomes more comfortable until the thought becomes habitual, making it increasingly difficult to break any resulting negative patterns, but easy to maintain the positive ones.

If our beliefs and habits are changed to weaken the connection and entity, it will eventually leave our presence but cannot be banished or destroyed and will have the potential to influence others and easily return to us. That is why the karma created from our thoughts is the most persevering and long lasting.

We can limit and control the potential and existing "clouds" of beings, created from the negative and errant thoughts of eight billion co-creators, by controlling our emotions and projecting positively.

Life After Life

Where did we come from, how did we get here, what is our purpose, and what happens after life? Physical science and the mythical explanations in religions do not seem to be much help in answering our biggest questions but perhaps that is best. What would be the point of our existence if we had all the answers? One of the most beneficial things I learned on my path is what is most important is not the destination, it's the journey. There are many logical theories addressing where we came from, how we got here and the extent of our purpose; however, it seems that definitive answers are simply not known. We touched on some of our reasons for being in this "physical" form and now I will describe some of the most interesting information I have found regarding what happens during and after what is known as death, which does not necessarily reflect my personal understandings and beliefs.

Once I was having a relevant conversation with a bright mind and had a revelation, right before they stated exactly what I was thinking, that began with my favorite two words, "What if what actually takes place after we leave the physical plane is governed or influenced by our individual beliefs?" Later I determined that to be at least partially true. When the body stops functioning, the pineal gland releases dimethyltryptamine (DMT), causing hallucinations and accounting for most near-death experiences. A process that could potentially lead us to believe that nothing further happens after life.

Tibetan Buddhists believe that the departed must realize and overcome their self-created delusions in order to smoothly transition to the afterlife or *reincarnation* (the rebirth of a soul in a new body). Monks, nuns and spiritual friends guide and comfort the soul and read specific excerpts from the Tibetan Book of the Dead during the *Bardo* (intermediate state), a transitional period of forty-nine days. They do not move or disturb the body for three to eight hours after breathing ceases as the soul can stay close to the corpse and become confused or upset, making the transition difficult and possibly changing the *realm* (ruled region) where the soul is reborn if it did not achieve karmic balance. From highest to lowest, the realms are Heaven, Human Life, Asura, Hungry Ghost, Animal Life, and Hell.

After the Bible edits, Heaven and Hell became permanent destinations in Christianity and the burden of balancing our karma was replaced with total forgiveness by confessing our sins and accepting Jesus. That causes believers to ignore accountability for their actions and inhibits balance and ascension.

Heaven is not a final destination in Buddhism; it is the peaceful realm above human life that is free of suffering and intended for those on the Noble Path and close to achieving harmonium. *Human Life* is the second highest realm, where we can enter Nirvana if we overcome all delusions. *Asura* is a spiritual realm of suffering frustration, as inhabitants are aware of what is taking place in and beyond the higher realms. *Hungry Ghost* is the realm where souls obsessed with consumption during human life can best balance their resulting negative karma through suffering attachment. *Animal Life* is a lower realm for those that caused excessive harm, committed acts of cruelty or killed animals (the punishment fits the crime here). *Hell* is also not a final destination; it is the realm for those with so much negative karma that they must suffer greatly and constantly in order to gain balance.

Most often the body is cremated or in some areas where wood is scarce, fed to the birds in a sky burial called *Jhator* (alms to the birds). Some monks prepared for ascension from their last incarnations by consuming elixirs and toxins to begin the process of mummification and preserve their final bodies. The organs were removed, and the bodies were covered with coal, wood and lime, and placed in a vessel surrounded by bricks for approximately three years. Then they were exhumed, painted, adorned with gold, and called Corporeal Bodhisattvas. But why preserve a dead body if it was only a shell?

Prominent people from many different cultures throughout history arranged for the preservation of their bodies and modern chemical mummification is quietly performed today, but not for resurrection. The purpose is to preserve their DNA and other valuable information. We will soon have, or possibly already have, the technology to clone human beings and reconnect them to their memories. That would allow a soul that has ascended beyond the realms of incarnation to maintain a physical presence in the lower dimensions; otherwise, and typically, they must choose reincarnation to have a physical presence. That is not to say that ancient civilizations were capable of cloning, but some had detailed knowledge of DNA, without the use of microscopes, and knew that the technology would exist in the distant future.

Jesus & Friends

This is probably a good place to reiterate that religious teachings and explanations are often mythical versions of actuality, and their colorful, symbolic descriptions can cause us to overlook the beautiful truths just below the surface and between the lines. All ancient philosophies, sciences and current legal and social systems recognize and are based on the fact that we are eternal souls and never actually die. The truth lies somewhere between the myths and non-belief and once accepted we begin to lose our fear of death and gain peace of mind that leads to a higher state of mind and greater appreciation of life. We only grieve when someone passes because we will miss them, and we accept all seemingly unfair circumstances because we understand that they are necessary for those affected to grow and balance.

Limited physical evidence and many logical hypotheses support the belief that spiritual teachers, such as Krishna, the Buddha, Jesus, Muhammad, and other enlightened souls, were indeed human beings. Seemingly more important than their physical existence is the extent to which the intended messages were changed or lost in the translations given to the masses.

There was a great culmination of spiritual knowledge around the time of Jesus Christ, about five hundred years after the Buddha, who apparently foretold the coming of Jesus, and about three thousand years after Krishna ruled the now-submerged island of Dwaraka near Gujarat, India around 3100 BCE. (Just in case, Before Common Era (BCE) and Before Christ (BC) are the same era, and *Anno Domini* (AD) means *in the year of the lord.*)

Knowledge is power and most people in powerful positions believe it is their responsibility to hide it. An effective method of propaganda is to leave most of a message intact and make changes to have the altered meaning suit the needs of the deceivers, and that is what happened to forgiveness.

It seems the intentional and unintentional misconceptions of most religious texts occur between the original written words and their interpretations, but any that choose to invest more time can exercise their ability to bypass the interpreters and arrive at their own conclusions as long as they have access. Passive forgiveness became the prominent biblical message after the edits in the year 325 AD to hide simple, empowering truths and persuade the oppressed to not retaliate against the oppressors.

For every action, there is an equal and opposing reaction. The Prophet Muhammad was born in Mecca, Saudi Arabia in the year 570 AD. About a year prior to his death in the year 632 AD, he began a preemptive conquest with the Christians at the town of Tabuk. Under only the threat of force, the head of the Ailah Tribe, Yahna bin Rawbah, peacefully consented and paid Muhammad the tribute, Al-Jizya, a tax for non-Muslims to serve as a reminder of Muslim rule and an incentive to convert to Islam.

Dhimmis (protected people), who based their beliefs on sacred texts, were allowed to practice their existing religions and Muhammad gave Yahna bin Rawbah the following letter of guarantee: "In the Name of Allah, the Most Beneficent, the Most Merciful. This is a guarantee of protection from Allah and Muhammad the Prophet, the Messenger of Allah, to Yahna bin Rawbah and the people of Ailah; their ships, their caravans on land and sea shall have the custody of Allah and the Prophet Muhammad, he and whosoever are with him of Ash-Sham people and those of the sea. Whosoever contravenes this treaty, his wealth shall not save him; it shall be the fair prize of him that takes it. Now it should not be lawful to hinder the men from any springs which they have been in the habit of frequenting, nor from any journeys they desire to make, whether by sea or by land."

The Muslims went on to conquer about two thirds of the Christian territories before their first defeat by Charles "The Hammer" Martel at the Battle of Poitiers in the village of Moussais-la-Bataille, France in the year 732 AD, and their first defense against the crusades was in the year 1095 AD. The holy war continues today, and the associated propaganda causes those religions to be the most misunderstood.

Before Muhammad began to rule other lands, he had to overcome the pagans in Mecca and convince them to stop worshiping multiple gods and worship the one god, Allah. With only the threat of force, he invoked Jihad, a concept and act that has been misused by numerous political and religious groups to justify their violence against the established Islamic order and mislead followers to overlook peaceful solutions with their perceived enemies. The verb, *jihad*, actually means strive or struggle and the ideal meaning Muhammad intended was *strive to improve*. As a noun, jihad does not mean "holy war", it is a diplomatic, legal or economic method of protecting the Islamic people and faith. Military Jihad is only used if there are no peaceful alternatives and must be justified by the proper authorities.

Eventually Christianity became the most popular religion in the world. Beyond having it forced upon them, some Muslims convert because they do not fully understand their own religion, and the idea of total forgiveness and eternal life in Heaven, by accepting a savior that died for their sins, can be very appealing to Buddhist and Hindu prospects burdened with the task of balancing their negative karma.

Forgiveness is a beautiful and powerful healing process, which we will address shortly, but forgiving karma seems illogical and there are different levels of passivity, which should be appropriated by the circumstances. The Christ Consciousness is a beautiful state of mind and if I become perplexed, I might ask myself; what would Jesus do? That would not necessarily determine my decision, as other philosophies come into play, but it would certainly be a factor, which is an example of incorporating the wisdom in religions without adhering to an organized religion or solidifying beliefs.

You do not have to be a Christian, Muslim, Hindu, or Buddhist to find beauty and wisdom in their teachings and philosophies, and we gain a much better perception by comparing them. Integrating our growing scientific knowledge assists us with interpreting and accepting the profound and difficult-to-perceive truths that our ancient ancestors discovered at the price of laborious efforts.

The Rosicrucian Society

What is your idea of success in life? The answer will tell you a lot about your current state of mind and level of awareness and it's a great way to measure progress. I have found that one key to success is having the wisdom to apply the right amount of pressure at the right time in any given situation. That seems steadfast for most earthly experiences, but what about the bigger picture and success for the soul?

The men and women of the Rosicrucian Society have been testing scientific and spiritual theories for hundreds of years. Their practical approach is not based on religion, and they have no *dogma*, which are *principles laid down by an authority as incontrovertibly true*. Some members are religious, and various religious groups have attached themselves, but the Rosicrucian objective is purely scientific.

The advanced and gifted researchers have awareness on the astral plane, and the society has collectively tested the laws of cycles and karma, as well as many other Universal Laws. They found and teach that developing a higher awareness allows us to move away from the world of effects and into the world of causes, taking control of our fate instead of being its pawn. Many wise and powerful people have been enlightened and empowered through the ever-evolving Rosicrucian philosophies.

Evidently, we return to physical bodies over and over again and only become free after we lose our personal desires and all essence of self in our thoughts and actions. Correct thoughts and actions for the purpose of rewards, such as good deeds done on Earth to receive riches in Heaven, will only result in reincarnation in order to receive those rewards.

"Every cause has its effect, every action its fruit, and desire is the cord that links them. When this thread is broken and burned out, the connection will end, and the soul will be free. True, you will continue to live and act, but no longer for the self. Thought of self will then be gone and consciousness will gradually merge into the Larger Life" - Joseph Weed.

Apparently, most souls enter an unconscious state of recovery after life, while severely unbalanced entities try to retain consciousness and rush to be reincarnated for the purpose of physical experiences. There are various states of consciousness during the transition and highly developed souls will pass in total awareness, eager to present themselves to what is known as the Board of Judgment and receive their appraisal, which is not a judgment of success and reward or failure and punishment. They evaluate every thought and action from the life and help determine the needs, location and duration of the soul's reincarnation to provide the highest probability of balancing and purifying the energies they affected.

Before reincarnation the soul may choose to do some of the work on the astral plane, and some are able to achieve balance there. Some religions portray this as a place of pain and punishment known as Purgatory, but no such things are present, and it's actually a plane of joyous effort and accomplishment. We choose many of the circumstances of our reincarnation, such as our parents and surroundings, based on what we want to accomplish and when we can achieve balance. We can also choose reincarnation after we balance our karma and purify the affected energies if we want to help and guide others on the physical plane but risk our balance and the possibility of having to go through the whole process again.

The soul enters the new body at first breath and initially retains awareness of its experiences and purpose but is unable to speak or comprehend. Sight and coordination are being developed and after a few weeks all focus shifts to operating the body, until a new personality emerges in roughly a year.

It is a huge blessing that most of us do not consciously recall past lives, as we might become overwhelmed with remorse and lose the desire to fulfill our purpose. It is the same mind defense mechanism that suppresses dreams. Some highly perceptive and otherwise trained people contend that we can attain the ability to vividly recall them; however, that could overwhelm us with regret and become a form of living in the past.

Most involuntary recalls occur between the ages of two and five years old and are often dismissed as hallucinations. There are thousands of compelling, documented cases of recalls, with incredible details that were convincingly confirmed, such as the experiences of Ryan Hammons and Dorothy Eady.

Most people's previous experiences remain in the subconscious and are evidenced by our talents and abilities, which seem to come easy, as well as some of our fears, passions and innate knowledge. A strong subconscious attachment to a past life could be the reason why some souls are unable to accept their current gender. Many phenomena are explained by the possibility that we have been here before.

Souls that achieve balance, purify all the energies they affected and choose to move into the higher dimensions can create a "heaven" of their own design, which is congruent with the idea that what takes place after life in the lower dimensions is governed or influenced by our individual beliefs.

Christo

Let's switch gears and explore a prominent example of symbolism in the Bible to give you an idea of how deep and different the underlying messages can be: The name, Christ, is derived from the Greek word, *christo*, which means *oil* and is symbolic of our reproductive oil in the resurrection story of Christ rising from the grave after three days. The hidden message is valuable instruction to increase our mental capacity, raise our consciousness level and reach enlightenment much sooner.

If not expelled from the body, our reproductive oil will begin to rise up the spinal column after three days, where it activates, stimulates and nourishes the pineal gland in the brain. Mainstream science claims that little is known about the pineal gland, but there is actually much information available if you choose to research. Now you know the main reason why some monks and other informed spiritualists practice celibacy. Fear not, you do not have to become a monk to experience the benefits. You can abstain for one week at a time and there is a specific week of the month, based on your birthday, when it is most beneficial.

Many have difficulty believing mythical stories, like the resurrection, but do so out of blind faith in their religion. Whether we believe the myths or not, we are robbed of the lessons in the underlying messages that were written for our benefit, unless we dig deeper and discover the intended meanings.

The Socratic Method

The basis of the Rosicrucian Society is that we should not accept anything as truth without some form of testing it ourselves and finding it to be true. The Buddha also strongly emphasized that necessity and I again ask you to not accept or dismiss any information herein without further exploration. We are barely scratching the surface of the seemingly controversial topics outlined in this short book and my intent is to spark interest and raise awareness- not impose limitations or influence conclusions.

It is up to you to determine the truth, and if you do not have firsthand knowledge, it can only be realized within you. Our educational system is solely based on memorization and critical thought is discouraged. What we routinely accept as facts are often products of debate, awarded to those with the best arguing skills, regardless of the logical and sometimes obvious conflicting facts and conditions.

The Socratic Method of discerning truth is quite simple: What do we know and *how* do we know? You will find that almost everything we think we know is not incontrovertibly true. The sun rises and sets every day. We know that because we experience it. American astronauts landed on the moon in the year 1969. Some know that to be true or false, the rest of us can only research and speculate. The astronauts stating that they landed on the moon does not make it true or untrue. Reading about it in a history book does not make it true or untrue. "All I know is that I know nothing" - Socrates.

Dependence

Long ago there was an emerging society, in which almost everyone had a purpose and contributed to the community to the best of their individual intelligence and abilities. Eventually the ones performing the more difficult and complicated tasks realized that the others were becoming increasingly dependent on them and collectively decided that their contribution was worth more. They commanded the others to build them elaborate accommodations and implemented their will through deception and secrecy.

Centuries passed as their wealth and control exponentially increased, until more than ninety percent of the wealth and resources were controlled by a tiny fraction of one percent of the community. I am obviously referring to our society, so how do we even begin to correct that and establish a fair and balanced existence? We must stop giving that elite fraction of our society our energy in every possible form and become less dependent in every aspect of our lives. There is no need to take any direct action against our oppressors. When enough of us stop giving them our energy, they will cease to exist.

"To err is human, to forgive is divine" - Alexander Pope

I was guilty of giving the ones I blamed for such circumstances power over me by resenting them because I had not yet discovered the spiritual philosophies described in this chapter. I also did not realize that everyone involved is at fault in such circumstances and part of the blame rests with me.

I began to take back control of my emotional energy by forgiving those perceived enemies after I realized that karma is always at work, we are all here to do what we're all here to do, and my only true enemy is my ego mind's projection of an enemy. I assure you that those people were not lying awake at night and worrying about what I thought of them. It was a one-sided affair, and the only way to regain my power and sanity was to forgive them and focus my energy on self-empowerment to become less dependent on the systems that allowed the elite to control every aspect of my life.

Then I began systematically and chronologically forgiving all other perceived enemies, working my way back through time and transforming decades of negative energy. It is a beautiful and comforting process, which allows us to apply critical thought and realize the necessity of our previous interactions. All interactions and relationships have specific purposes to benefit the participants' growth and balance.

Once we become aware of the necessity and begin practicing the process of forgiveness, we often find that the most difficult person to forgive is ourselves. Realizing the err of our ways and the resulting negative effects we caused along our journey to a higher level of awareness and compassion can weigh heavily on the soul. We must apply the same philosophies and wisdom to ourselves as we do to others we no longer wish to resent. Accept the fact that we cannot change the past and embrace the truth that with each new day we are born again and have the opportunity to change the future.

Chapter Four

Empowerment

The images and information received through the James Webb Space Telescope launched in the year 2022 are amazing. The biggest discovery to date is the Big Bang either did not occur or happened much sooner, spawning many new theories. Looking across space is looking across time and we expected to find the Universe in its infant state thirteen billion years ago but discovered galaxies larger and apparently older than the Milky Way Galaxy.

The Standard Model is another theory that mainstream science adopted as fact and later determined to be inconclusive. This is the stuff I love to think about and explore possibilities when I get to the point of less certainty, where we must accept that we might not find the answers instead of concluding.

Understanding that the act of looking, with the expectation of seeing something, is what creates something to see; how does that affect what was seen with the telescope? Whose expectations and act of observation decided what could be seen or was it previously created by our collective mind?

A theory that we exist in a computerized simulation provides some insight into Quantum Mechanics, as it is based on similar principles, one of the exceptions being that in a simulation there is a controller and through Quantum Mechanics our collective consciousness is in control. The entire landscape of a simulation does not exist where we are not participating, the parts are rendered as we approach them.

We have never approached the parts we are rendering now and are likely seeing what our collective mind expects to find, which could mean that a critical amount of the population does not believe in an expanding Universe. Perhaps enough of us realize that our consciousness is what is actually expanding. The theories of the god particle and dark matter being the unseen forces that create and govern the Universe are modern attempts to physically explain what the ancients knew; we create and govern the Universe.

As much as I have enjoyed watching my childhood comic books come to life, many of the newer films revolve around the Multiverse Theory, which we can neither prove nor disprove, but the Many Worlds Theory, derived from Quantum Theory, goes beyond Quantum Fact. There are not necessarily infinite versions of the physical you; there are infinite versions of the you that manifest in one physical reality, all existing at the same time in the higher dimensions, which are less dense than our physical plane. Our individual thoughts (upward causation) create multiple possible realities, which are reduced to probable realities and one physical reality by our collective thought and choice (downward causation). A multiverse goes well beyond those mechanics, with individual choices manifesting multiple realities.

We found our way back to Quantum Mechanics because we are in the chapter of empowerment and there is no better way to empower yourself. Introducing the basic concept and application is the main purpose of this book and my wish is that you will pursue it further, until you realize your power. As those who control the media convince us of what *is* reality, and our projection of that perception creates reality; who has your power now?

The Powers That Be

The powers that be (PTB) really like their acronyms. I remember reading about the virus that came to be cleverly named COVID back in the year 2012. Many of us were experiencing the spiritual awakening and increased awareness the Mayans foretold, and information was increasingly available to help us find the answers to our questions. The first thing I learned when I began searching for the truth was to follow the money, and that is all we must do to discover who are behind such mass efforts to control and reduce the population. Money is only part of control and there are multiple agendas.

HIV, Human Immunodeficiency Virus, was designed in a laboratory and listed under a U.S. patent. DARPA, Defense Advanced Research Projects Agency, the unaccountable DOD corporation that created Agent Orange, now has a four-billion-dollar annual budget. HAARP, High-frequency Active Auroral Research Program, triggers the occurrence of natural disasters and intensifies them with ELF, Extremely Low Frequencies.

There are numerous methods to reduce the population, and we could view them as an IQ test. You can take measures to overcome anything the PTB throw at you if you are aware of your true surroundings. So, what should you do; get mad, get even or get smart? One works and the others only distract us.

The first step in overcoming the assault on our health through our air, water, food, and medication is also the first step in becoming less dependent.

That is to begin to take control of your health and well-being. You can do it because you must. One informed step at a time, you will become your best advisor. That does not mean that you go it alone. No one can succeed without the help and support of others. What I am suggesting is to privately question everything you are told, do your own research to become aware of all factors, remedies and probable outcomes, and remain open to all viable options.

Holistic

Holistic is defined as *encompassing all interconnecting parts of the whole.* Holistic health encompasses the mind, body and spirit as a whole. Being that all possibilities exist in the higher dimensions of the spiritual realm, we will begin with spiritual health and the Human Chakra System:

Chakra is a Sanskrit word meaning *wheel* and refers to the energy centers of the human body that receive and transform *Prana* (life force), which is the primal source of all energy manifested in various frequencies. There are thousands of minor chakras, forty secondary chakras, and seven primary chakras. *Nadi* is a Sanskrit word meaning *pipe* or *vein.* The nadis transport prana throughout the energy system.

Blockages or poor function in the system result in mental and physical issues, which can be corrected by taking measures to open or purify the chakras to induce or restore harmonious function. The seven primary chakras are located up the spinal column in the order of the visible light spectrum.

The Root Chakra is located behind the genitals and is red in color. It opens downward and connects to the physical world, allowing earthly energies to enter the body. Proper function results in a harmonious relationship with Nature and grounds the vibrations of the higher chakras. Improper function causes our thoughts and actions to revolve around material possessions, security and overindulgence.

The Sacral Chakra is located above the genitals and is orange in color. It opens forward, influences the desire to create and procreate, and receives and nourishes the energies that permeate Nature. Proper function allows us to be creative and open to others of the opposite sex. Improper function misdirects our creative sexuality and leads to uncertainty, low self-esteem, depression, and sexual tension.

The Solar Plexus Chakra is located above the navel and is gold in color. It opens forward and is directly connected to the astral body. Solar energy is absorbed to nurture the ethereal bodies and energize the physical body, and our emotional energy resonates here. This is the seat of our will, where the desires from the lower chakras are controlled and purified to allow the higher chakras to manifest positive outcomes. Proper function permits peace, harmony, acceptance, and the ability to perceive the vibrations of others. Improper function creates the desire to control and manipulate the outside world in accordance with our will and misuse our power, while we often find obstacles, uncertainty and dissatisfaction.

The Heart Chakra is located at the center of the chest and is green in color, with a secondary color of pink. It opens forward and connects the lower (physical and emotional) chakras to the upper (mental and spiritual) chakras. Proper function allows us to project specific, controlled emotions to the Source in order to improve the conditions around us, attune to Nature and experience unconditional love. Improper function misguides participatory manifestation, disconnects us from our true nature and ability to receive love, and hinders our ability to give freely by expecting something in return.

The Throat Chakra is located just below the larynx and is light blue in color. It opens forward, is connected to a secondary chakra that opens to the rear and is the center of communication, expression and inspiration. Proper function allows us to express ourselves and to speak and discern truth. Improper function creates distrust and a looming feeling of guilt, while fear of judgment prevents self-expression.

The Third Eye Chakra is located above the brow and is indigo in color, with a secondary color of yellow. It opens forward, is the seat of our mental power and controls the central nervous system. Opening the third eye is a conscious developmental process, evidenced by a compelling pursuit of holistic scientific research and confirmation of philosophies and theories that once appeared mythical. Many of the possibilities previously overlooked come to light and we eventually perceive the forces at work that create the physical world and attain the necessary wisdom to control those energies. An under-developed third eye keeps us grounded in the physical world and controlled by our ego minds.

The Crown Chakra is located at the top of the head and is violet in color. It opens upward and is seated in the pineal gland. This is the source of prana for all the chakras and our connection to the higher dimensions, where we are influenced by the Divine and accept the responsibility of co-creators. A completely opened crown chakra ceases to absorb external energy and begins to radiate its own energy, which forms a crown of ethereal light above the head that is symbolized by Jesus's halo. If not developed, we often remain imprisoned by fear and separated from the abundance of the Universe.

Only the three lower chakras are active in the average person, and they will be purified as the Heart Chakra opens, which is the first step. Next is the third eye, then the crown and the throat is last. Opening and restoring the chakra system requires a bit of self-education and devotion. It is a very rewarding and empowering experience that can only be achieved through meditation.

A Quiet Mind Can Weather Any Storm

Energy is literally information. Difficult to visualize... maybe think of looking through Neo's eyes in the film, The Matrix, which is a metaphorical work of art. We are particles of all waves of information but are unable to utilize this energy until we are able to perceive and receive it. The Law of Descending Energy states that when we are exposed to lower vibrations, our energy depletes and when we are exposed to higher vibrations, we receive energy. As our chakras and minds open, we gain access to an abundance of energy and must make time for our minds to quietly process the information.

The Standardized Effect states that all past, present and future information, creations and ideas are currently existing, and we are only realizing them. The greatest minds in history had their ideas "come to them" while dreaming or in a meditative state because their minds were quiet and open to receive.

We use just as much energy with our brains as we do with our bodies. Errant thoughts lead to racing minds, and we often find ways to distract ourselves in an attempt to quiet the mind. If you always need ambient noise, such as music and television, to be comfortable, it is an indicator that you will greatly benefit from learning how to control errant thoughts without such distractions. Eventually you will appreciate the silence and associated relief and will no longer need ambient noise to help you stabilize.

We find many ways to achieve temporary peace through hobbies, games and sports that require our complete attention, which is why they are so rewarding. It's an escape from our relentless problems, duties and errant thoughts. I relied on playing guitar or exercising to relieve stress and refocus before discovering that there is another means that can be practiced almost anywhere and anytime.

Meditation can be as simple or complicated as you decide. Even if you do not pursue any specific exercises to develop your chakras, practicing various forms of focused meditation is extremely beneficial to your mental and physical health, and some of the chakra development happens naturally.

Transcendental meditation is a widely practiced form created by Maharishi Mahesh Yogi, and one of the easier methods to achieve the fourth state of consciousness; transcending wake, sleep and dream. You simply concentrate on a *mantra*, a Sanskrit word meaning *mind vehicle*, and repeat it for twenty minutes, twice a day or when convenient and as circumstances allow. I rarely mind short waits in lines or waiting rooms where I can meditate. The last time I went to an appointment I was told there was a twenty-minute wait. They were ready sooner than expected and I asked for a few more minutes.

You can also choose an object or color on which to concentrate, with your eyes open or closed, depending on the situation and what works best for you. This seems to be the best way for most people to begin practicing, by simply focusing on one thing and keeping all other thoughts out of mind.

We naturally learn how to use the mind to control the body, but we must also learn how to control the mind because it can certainly get in the way. "Your soul has a special mission. Your soul is supremely conscious of it. Maya, illusion or forgetfulness, makes you feel that you are finite, weak and helpless. That is not true. You are not the body. You are not the senses. You are not the mind. These are all limited. You are the soul, which is unlimited" - Sri Chinmoy.

Breathe Mindfully

Breathing is crucial to your metaphysical health, and you will find many beneficial exercises as you begin to explore various forms of meditation. We can bring prana into our chakras, just as we bring air into our lungs, and focusing on your breath is another simple way to begin practicing. Most of the time you will be inhaling faster than exhaling, which allows you to absorb more energy in the same way that more oxygen can be absorbed by releasing the breath slowly. You can incorporate other exercises as you progress, such as mantras and guided thought, but most start by envisioning their breath as white light entering and exiting the body. Quiet surroundings are initially preferred, and you will eventually be able to block out all ambient noise and distractions to allow you to enter the meditative state.

Binaural frequencies can greatly enhance and accelerate the benefits of meditation by placing different frequencies in each ear, through ear buds or headphones, to achieve central frequencies with specific purposes. Listening to meditation music and other genres, when possible, in 432 hertz instead of 440 hertz also enhances and accelerates progress. 432 hertz is the frequency of our bodies and instruments were tuned accordingly for millennia, until the American Standards Association forced the change in the year 1936. It's another widespread method of keeping us out of balance and synchronicity.

Gemstones and precious metals are great for meditation, healing and overcoming obstacles. Formed over millions of years, they hold and transmit information collected during formation, with various uses and benefits. There are crystals to assist with any condition or scenario, and it only takes one positive experience to become “hooked” as I did. Many successful people are or were avid collectors, such as J.P. Morgan, who had a stone named after him; Morganite. Gold is the metal of masculine energy and silver is feminine. We benefit from and prefer the one that compensates for any deficiencies.

Energy healing is an internal technology that you can develop through meditation. I have several firsthand experiences; otherwise, I would not be professing such a thing. For example, a close friend had her first shoulder surgery just before I began learning how to heal with intent. After her surgery on the other shoulder, I combined the fifth mode of prayer with mindful breathing and visualized her as “completely healed”, with that as the mantra, then felt immense gratitude that it was indeed reality.

That was performed for about ten minutes each night for a week; although, specific times and the duration are not crucial factors. The critical component is always achieving certainty of the desired reality as actuality without attachment to outcome. Her shoulder healed more than twice as fast as the first one and her doctor was thrilled but could not provide an explanation for the quick recovery. I was also thrilled but have kept it to myself to this day.

Reiki and most forms of energy healing are methods to change the energy the atoms that comprise a being are in through attunement. The practitioner achieves and maintains a high vibration and the beneficiary's frequency attunes to the higher vibration, removing blockages and negative energy. It is often most powerful when within someone's energy circle but can also be done from a remote location. Healing oneself works differently, as we must attune to a higher frequency in order to raise our own. Attunement is easily evidenced by placing clocks, pendulums or electric motors very close to each other. They will align their frequencies to cycle in unison, and women close to each other naturally align their menstrual cycles over time.

The difference in being successful or unsuccessful in any practice is the difference between faith and hope. If we only hope that something will happen, we send the message that it is not happening. If we have faith and achieve the feeling that our wish is reality, we send the message that it is.

* Nikola Tesla's 3-6-9 meditation is a ritualistic method of healing and manifestation: Envision three desired outcomes and achieve the feeling that they are reality six times a day for nine seconds each.

Laughter Is The Best Medicine

Our level of vibration increases when we receive good news or accomplish a goal, sometimes too much, which is known as an over-positive condition. After things calm down, we often crash hard into a lower frequency before returning to our base frequency. Our level of vibration decreases when we receive disturbing news or experience failure, and sometimes we do not swing back to our base frequency, lowering the base frequency over time. A wise objective is to gradually raise our vibration and sustain the higher level, but some of us swing back and forth on an emotional roller coaster and remain unaware of what is taking place.

Laughter truly is the best medicine for a negative condition. Beautiful scenery, music, fragrances, and other positive stimulation of the senses are also beneficial. There are ways to permanently raise your vibration, and there are ways to avoid the adverse effects of an over-positive condition. Here are some effective meditative exercises you can use to gradually vibrate at a higher level and attain harmonium:

It takes about two hours to notice the subtle effects, and you can repeat as often as desired. I like to do each one daily, at least once, to maintain harmonium. The exercise to balance an over-positive condition also enhances the body's defense system and aids in combating harmful microorganisms. It should be done every two hours after cold and flu-type symptoms occur, and daily to help avoid them. Always achieve at least a light meditative state before beginning, heavier when possible but not so deep that you lose focus. One method is to visualize hot pink for one minute to open the heart, sky blue for one minute to stimulate the upper chakras, and bright white for one minute to cleanse thought.

* To counteract a negative condition and raise your level of vibration: Sit with your back straight, feet apart, rest your palms upward on your thighs, and bring your thumbs and middle fingers together. Relax all possible muscles while keeping your back straight and fingers together. Breathe out, inhale slowly and completely, then hold your breath in for a count of seven. Exhale slowly and completely, then take one or two consistent breaths and identically repeat the process six times for a total of seven. Each count is about a second or less and be consistent with the timing.

You can include visualization of translucent colors at each of the seven chakra sites as you progress, starting with the violet crown, then the indigo third eye, sky blue throat, green heart, gold solar plexus, orange sacral, and red root. You can bring the colors into your body from head to toe as you breathe in, then bring in white light from toe to head and out through the selected chakra to cleanse it. That is not necessary to counteract a negative condition and should only be included after you have mastered the exercise. It's just an opportunity to combine the process with some chakra stimulation.

* To counteract an over-positive condition and boost your immunity: Sit with your back straight, feet together, and bring your fingers together in front of your chest. Relax all possible muscles while keeping your back straight with your feet and fingers still together. Breathe in, exhale slowly and completely, then hold your breath out for a count of five. Inhale slowly and completely, then take one or two consistent breaths and identically repeat the process four times for a total of five.

That should be done as soon as possible after achieving an extremely positive condition, and every two hours when possible or as needed, which will keep you from crashing into a lower frequency. You can also bring light into your body while inhaling after you have mastered the exercise.

* A quick way to bring positive energy into your physical and ethereal bodies is to stand straight, with your feet apart and arms to your side, lightly

clinch your jaw and fists, and relax the rest of your body. Inhale slowly and completely to a count of five, then exhale slowly and completely to a count of ten. Repeat nine times for a total of ten, bringing in light or adding other visualizations as you progress. It can also be performed while seated.

These are three simple exercises you can use to help stimulate and cleanse your chakras every day: Sit with your back straight and feet apart, rest your palms upward on your thighs, and bring your thumbs and middle fingers together for each of these exercises, then achieve a light meditative state.

* The root and sacral chakras are affected by exhaling and holding the breath out, contracting the anus, as if suppressing a bowel movement, then contracting the bladder area, as if suppressing urination. Gently hold them in for a count of three and repeat twice for a total of three times.

* The solar plexus and heart chakras are affected by exhaling and holding the breath out, bringing the upper abdomen up and slightly under the ribs, then gently pushing the upper body outward for a count of three and repeating twice for a total of three times. Try not to strain with any of these.

* The throat, third eye and crown chakras are affected by exhaling and holding the breath out, raising the shoulders up and compressing the neck for a count of three. Repeat twice for a total of three times. Project translucent colors during, and white light after, each exercise at each area to enhance.

We must believe in the process of all meditative exercises and not become discouraged or give up if we do not experience immediate results. The effects often take time to manifest, and while some will naturally excel due to their belief in positive results and ability to focus, some will need to develop those beliefs and abilities in order to experience positive results. Eventually you will be able to remain calm in situations that were previously unsettling, engage in critical thought in lieu of replaying old emotional occurrences, release all negative energy and attachments, and experience harmonium.

"He who has peace of mind disturbs neither himself nor another" - Bruce Lee

Psychosis?

Most involuntary spiritual awakenings occur in gifted children between the ages of ten and fourteen. Yogis and others practice for years to hear inner voices and see into the higher dimensions, many of them unsuccessful in achieving what happens naturally in gifted children. Indigenous cultures embrace the process and place the child in the care of a mentor, who trains them to control and utilize their gift. Modern cultures totally freak out if their children hear voices or hallucinate. The child is placed in the care of a psychiatrist, who diagnoses, medicates and attempts to suppress their gift. That never works and many are labeled as psychotic and institutionalized, which often limits or destroys their futures.

There are physical circumstances where medications are required, such as chemical imbalances and inner voices commanding violent or unhealthy behavior. There are limited and temporary applications for medication, but most often we should replace the "c" with a "t" and choose meditation.

Reticent?

I felt very different and alone and did not realize that I was "normal" until discovering that being introverted is not necessarily a *bad* thing. In fact, it has proven to be an advantage in many previous experiences, and even more so with the interests I am currently pursuing.

Our society rewards extroverts and leads us to believe that something is wrong with us if we are not outgoing and comfortable with crowds, loud noise and frequent distraction. Many people are overly concerned with broadcasting their every move on social media in an attempt to satisfy their need for approval and obtain validation, projecting their values onto others.

Introverts naturally direct their energy to where it is best utilized and are often more in tune with their surroundings. Begin to turn your attention inward and you will begin to know thyself. "You are the Universe in ecstatic motion. Yesterday I was clever, so I wanted to change the world. Today I am wise, so I am changing myself. What you seek is seeking you" - Rumi. The last line of that quote can certainly be applied to the Law of Attraction, but when taken as a whole, we can see that the intended message is; what you are searching for is what is conducting the search.

Fight Or Flight

Stress is an internal condition, caused by our inability to deal with external issues. Blaming others for our stress is like blaming the Sun when we get burned and acceptance of circumstances is necessary to help prevent it.

Realizing what is taking place is half the task, so let's uncover the source:

High amounts of adrenaline are released into the body in dangerous situations, which our ancestors often needed to defend themselves or flee from wild animals. In fact, we are designed to elevate our adrenaline levels in anticipation of danger. Our heart rate increases, and the senses become more acute, while nutrients and blood flow are directed away from the organs and used to sustain muscular activity. That was critical in prehistoric times and still necessary today, in limited situations, but now many people induce the fight or flight mechanism on a regular basis in every aspect of their lives.

Some of the external issues we experience can be difficult or impossible to resolve, and we can easily slip into periodic or continuously active states of high adrenaline production, which shifts the body's focus and energy away from the immune, digestive, circulatory, and neurological systems.

Stress is eliminated as our ability to deal with external situations improves. The first step is realizing and accepting the fact that our challenges are happening for specific reasons, and they will persist until we address them. Ignoring, suppressing and avoiding our external issues only prolongs and escalates them. When we internalize and tell ourselves we're fine, without discovering why things are happening, we miss the opportunity to learn from them and often release our anger and frustration onto others, which is compounded by judging and trying to control external conditions without considering karma.

Breathing exercises alleviate stressful situations and a quiet mind helps prevent stress from occurring. Acceptance, forgiveness, meditation, critical thought, self-awareness, empathy, and compassion are required to overcome an inherent reaction that has evolved to do more harm than good.

The Placebo Effect

If you excelled at organized sports, one of your coaches probably taught you what my father taught me; to envision success in the task at hand. Whether seeing the ball go in the goal or crossing the finish line, only those that truly believe it will happen are able to make it happen. The most successful people have been taught or instinctively know this "secret" and are not hindered by doubt because that would prevent them from achieving their goals. The process is a derivative of the fifth mode of prayer.

Many synthesized medications are formulated to trigger specific reactions in the brain, in which various glands release chemicals to alleviate the symptoms. Your mind can command your brain to do the same thing, by believing the desired result is happening in what is called the Placebo Effect.

Basically, all that is required for a new drug to be approved for public distribution is that it does not contain banned ingredients or kill you instantly, and it must outperform a *placebo*, which is *a harmless pill, medicine or procedure prescribed more for the psychological benefit to the patient than the physiological effect*. The psychological benefit of the belief that the condition will improve is so strong that many drugs do not pass the test, and most approved medications narrowly outperform the placebo.

I remember a nurse that was working with a doctor to get a patient off a pain medication, as her injury had properly healed, and they believed it was no longer needed. She quickly became unable to cope and repeatedly demanded that they refill the prescription. The doctor prescribed a placebo and told her it was a new drug that was very effective, but highly addictive, and should only be taken when absolutely necessary to avoid becoming dependent. They did not hear from her until the next checkup, when she explained that the medication had effectively relieved the pain, and a refill was not requested.

In the year 2002 doctors Bruce Moseley and Baruch Brody performed a study, in which 180 patients with knee pain underwent arthroscopic surgery. Sixty of the procedures were simulated; small incisions were made, but no instruments were inserted, and no cartilage was removed. After monitoring them for two years, none of the patients that underwent the actual surgery reported less pain or better function than the placebo patients, who surprisingly reported better outcomes in some cases. The doctors found that the same therapeutic benefits of the surgery can be achieved with non-invasive placebo surgery.

This is the "beliefs" part of diet, habits and beliefs, and the reason I do not create doubt in someone's process if they believe it is improving their condition, unless it's something obviously ineffective or harmful. Their belief is often more important than the actual treatment. With "properly" prescribed and taken pharmaceutical drugs being the number one cause of death in the United States, it seems that many would greatly benefit from realizing and developing their innate ability to heal through belief.

Reverse Value System

I know several couples that have lots of money and everything they desire. They remodeled their kitchens or designed their new construction to have the most expensive appliances and fixtures, granite counter tops and oak cabinets. Each of them stocked their elaborate kitchens with the cheapest and most toxic food they could buy, unwittingly adhering to the reverse value system our society follows.

Nothing is more important and valuable than what we put in our bodies, but that is where most people cut corners, regardless of their income. Being so backwards and widespread, we might never question it without having it brought to our attention. Even if we completely disregard our health, it is still costing much more in the long run, with the resulting co-pays and other medical bills that are a direct result of skimping on our food. It is a simple choice; pay for good food now or pay the doctors a lot more later.

I am trying to minimally include my personal successes; however, to help assure you that the right organic foods, exercise and state of mind (diet, habits & beliefs) are the keys to good health, I testify that I have not visited any doctors, except for injuries and checkups, in my adult life and I'm old.

The only medication I took, other than antibiotics, was for allergies. I thought I had become allergic to pollen in my early thirties because I had not yet improved my diet to exclude the toxins that had built up in my system, lowered my immunity and permitted the condition. A few weeks after doing so I was able to stop taking the medication and the only allergic reactions I have experienced were food related.

Cell Toxicity

You will not only save money on medical bills; you will feel much better and have more energy. The body uses energy to digest food but should not become lethargic and require or induce sleep during the process. That is caused by diversion of cell energy to fight the consumed toxins, which build up over time and overwork the body's defense system, lower immunity and result in various forms of disease.

Envision or draw a small circle and shade the lower hemisphere. The circle represents one of the billions of cells that comprise our bodies and the shaded area is the toxicity level. Let's suppose that we are born with a cell toxicity level of fifty percent, which could be much more or less, depending on the amount of toxins versus nutrients consumed by our mother, as well as her habits and environment. As years pass, we either decrease or increase our toxicity level until we become increasingly healthy or ill.

The cells are amazingly resilient and able to minimize most adverse effects until they reach a toxicity level of ninety percent and can no longer defend themselves (shade in all but ten percent of the circle). That is when symptoms become much stronger and various diseases, such as Parkinson's, Alzheimer's, cancer, type two diabetes, and heart disease are diagnosed. Unfortunately, medications are often prescribed to treat the symptoms, the root cause is rarely addressed, and the "disease" ends the life. Alternatively eliminating all possible toxins and consuming raw, nutrient-dense foods and beverages will eventually reverse most conditions, and all or most toxic medications will no longer be needed.

Cancer cells cannot live in a healthy environment. They thrive on sugar, acidity and a low oxygen level. A healthy, low-sugar, alkaline diet and corresponding lifestyle is the only actual "cure". The American Cancer Society does not recognize a healthy diet and habits as a cure. They claim they are still searching and need our donations to fund research and their industry. In the 1930s Dr. Max Gerson proved that the body's cells will heal themselves after the toxins are removed by adhering to a strict diet and regimen. It is not found in any medical journal because nutritional healing decreases the cancer industry's profits, and it is classified as nutrition- not medicine. That also applies to the medical industry's treatment of disease.

Most synthetic medications are highly toxic to the cells and are derived and synthesized from natural plant sources, which are what we should be consuming to solve the problems without the side effects, but there is no profit in that. So, we are led to believe that there is something incurably wrong with us or we have inherited the conditions of our ancestors to keep us sick and dependent on their poisons.

The Hippocratic Oath

"With regard to healing the sick, I will devise and order for them the best diet, according to my judgment and means; and I will take care that they suffer no hurt or damage. Nor shall any man's entreaty prevail upon me to administer poison to anyone; neither will I counsel any man to do so."

What might the founder of modern medicine think about what is taking place today? I imagine that he would be more than frustrated to witness so many people unwittingly suffering for profit. I reiterate that most of the people within big industries are not *bad* or *evil*, in this case I am referring to doctors and their staffs, but they have been qualified (reduced and limited) to generate profits for their industry.

There is an increasing number of medical doctors that are learning to heal with nutrition, which is a very powerful and effective method when combined with their incredible diagnostic capabilities. We need doctors and their staffs for monitoring, trauma and surgery; however, we need them to learn how to heal illness with nutrition and put our health before profits, which is a tough thing to realize when they are in medical school. The amount of information they must memorize and recall leaves little or no time to question the information or think for themselves, which often becomes standard practice. They are less likely to consider any future information that is not sourced through the medical industry.

I have a friend that was able to stop taking allergy medications. He told his sister-in-law, who is a medical doctor, that he no longer needed them because he had eliminated the toxins from his diet that were causing the problem. She immediately stated that he should try a newly released allergy medicine because it was the best. He again stated that he no longer had allergies and asked why he should take anything if the problem was solved. She just looked at him curiously and it became obvious that she could not grasp the concept of eliminating the symptoms of a condition without medication, which is all they are trained to use. It's the only method most of them know and difficult for them to see beyond.

That is the case for all conditions and diseases that can be reversed with our diets, habits and beliefs. Everything we put in our bodies has a huge impact on our health, especially when the cell toxicity level rises above ninety percent. The way to become healthy is to treat the source- not the symptoms.

The same friend wanted to be freed from his prescribed medications and determined that it should be done under the supervision of the right doctor. He went to visit his existing doctor and was told that once he started taking blood pressure medications, he would be on them for the rest of his life. He had the presence of mind to question that response and did so by asking, "If the source of the problem has been removed and there are no longer any symptoms to treat, why is the medication still necessary?"

His doctor had no answer and became frustrated as he pondered this 180-degree information, which was opposite of his training and beliefs, but his instincts and common sense could not deny. He told my friend that he would not oversee the process of getting off the drugs and he should find another doctor. So, he did and was eventually able to stop taking all forms of synthetic medications, a process that can be difficult for some and requires a holistic approach, often with drastic lifestyle changes.

Many will still prefer to take a pill, relieve the symptoms and suffer the consequences after realizing that they can heal themselves with self-education and dedication. Try not to view it as something that must be done all at once. In most cases, gradual changes and the right substitutions are the best path to success; however, all changes need to be made quickly if your cell toxicity level is over ninety percent.

The Motivational Triad

Dr. Douglas Lisle spent over twenty years studying the causes behind our desires. We were aware of the *pursuit of pleasure* and *avoidance of pain*, and he discovered that the *conservation of energy* was the overlooked third incentive. He uses the example of a predator, such as a shark, seeking food and sex without sustaining injury, and the additional incentive is ease of acquisition. The shark will use less energy if he pursues closer and larger prey, and the larger the prey, the more satisfying the experience.

We are wired the same way and remaining unaware of the third incentive inhibits us from taking control of our desires, specifically our food and beverage choices. Our taste buds do not exist to bring us pleasure; they exist to tell us which foods are richest in calories. It was important for our ancient ancestors to get the most calories from each meal, as they were often few and far between. Today we seek pleasure from food that is high in calories but rarely miss meals, which creates a huge issue.

Your taste buds are extremely sensitive. If you pick an apple and let it ripen for one day, it will taste sweeter than one you pick and eat the same day. Your taste buds will tell you to eat the sweet one, like you'll never get another, even if you have an apple tree, and it's up to you to tame them. Our food and beverages are to provide nutrients and energy- not bring us pleasure, but we can find a happy medium.

I thought that I had switched to a healthy breakfast, by eating organic granola, berries and seeds with coconut milk, but I forgot to consider the added sugar. The same was true with my "healthy" beverage alternatives, such as my favorite aloe water, which had a ridiculous amount of processed sugar. So, I switched to organic, raw, unheated oats and unsweetened coconut milk, with vanilla for flavor, and added a tablespoon of organic honey to sweeten the mix, then went to work on my beverage selection.

The Regulators

While we're on the subject of breakfast, a hundred years ago most Americans ate a light morning meal, consisting of coffee, juice, toast, and sometimes cereal, especially if they worked in an office and did not expend a lot of energy, until the Beech-Nut Packaging Company hired Edward Bernays to con the public into eating bacon for breakfast. He sought out physicians that would back the campaign, and they added eggs and published their opinions in newspapers and magazines. While eggs are arguably beneficial in moderation for some diets, we definitively know that bacon is extremely unhealthy for all diets, but many still regularly consume.

From 1946 to 1952, R.J. Reynolds paid the medical industry to support an advertising campaign with the slogan, "More doctors smoke Camels than any other cigarette". When I ask people in the medical industry and those older than me how that could happen, they all reply, "We didn't know any better".

There were those that knew better, and the only way they could delay the truth and minimize the effect was to associate themselves with an organization that could profit as much or more. There are countless misconceptions and injustices that we eventually realized and shamefully corrected because the ones we entrust to truthfully advise and protect us historically and currently do the exact opposite.

A blatant example of deception for profit in modern times is the continuously rising recommended daily allowance of protein listed on many manufacturers' labels, which has mysteriously increased from fifty to over eighty grams per day. Although the FDA RDA remains unchanged for decades, they allow it to happen, which creates unnecessary health issues, specifically pancreatic cancer because the organ becomes overwhelmed and cannot process the recommended amount many people believe they need.

The FDA does not perform independent testing of any food or drug. They base their approval on the manufacturers' test results, which is one of the scariest arrangements anyone could ever imagine. There is an established false belief that the "government" uses our tax dollars to protect consumers from toxic products and conditions with regulatory agencies, but they are corporations, funded by the companies they regulate. If you ask anyone that sought justice for any related offense, you will find that it was denied or tied up in litigation until it was no longer relevant, or the plaintiffs passed away.

Many years ago, a very bright and young EPA agent came to my home to buy a chair that I had listed for sale. She commented on how close the power lines were to some of the houses in the neighborhood. I was intrigued when she mentioned the possibility of electromagnetic pollution and asked what could be done about it. She explained that it was an existing condition with a huge gray area and was beyond their control. EPA agents are not authorized to initiate investigations; they can only respond to complaints.

No regulatory authority is looking out for you, as much as some agents would like to. In most cases of illness from approved foods, beverages and medications, all liability ultimately falls to the consumer, and environmental offenders pay to play. The only solution is to educate and protect ourselves.

be CAWFUL and don't be a DAWFUS

My corniest acronyms ever, but they remind me that with clean air, water & food you live, and with dirty air, water & food you suffer. When I say live, I mean vibrantly, full of energy and passion because you choose quantity and quality of life, as opposed to just "quality". The toxic foods and beverages that you crave and believe you cannot live without will no longer be appealing to you after introducing the healthy alternatives that make you feel better, and you will begin to crave them. When I say suffer, I mean relentlessly, with exponentially decreasing energy, health, time, and the ability to enjoy life.

There is not much we can do about the toxins in our outside air, other than eliminating the sources; however, we can improve the air quality in our homes and offices, which allows us to breathe cleaner air when there. Purchase the very best filters for the return air on your HVAC system and replace them regularly. They are expensive, but it's a part of the pay more now or pay much more later philosophy. There are HVAC systems available that provide ultraviolet light and electrostatic filtration, and you can utilize air purifiers that have HEPA filters and, more importantly, provide deionization, where negatively charged particles are released and attach to positively charged particles, and they fall to the ground.

Plastic is not an oxygen barrier. Toxic vapors from household and lawn chemicals seep into ambient air and impact our health. They should be stored in an airtight container, in a garage or basement, and away from people and pets. Notice that most supermarkets place their chemicals on the pet food aisle, maybe because our pets are unable to notice and complain about the toxins in their food and water.

Furry Friends

The reverse value system is also evidenced by the typical food choices for our pets. We rarely make the association between the processed foods they seem to like, with no irregularity or other apparent issues, and their gradually declining health, which can result in recurring vet visits without resolution.

No animal (or human) can remain healthy by eating nutrient-depleted, enzyme-less processed food, and there is no simple or inexpensive solution, until compared to the eventual expense and lost time. A wild animal eats their prey immediately after the kill. They get proteins, nutrients and enzymes that are still "alive", and their systems recognize, accept and process them. Our bodies work the same way, but we are not carnivores. All meat-eating animals have short and straight digestive tracts, much unlike human beings.

It might seem like you do not have the time and money to research and provide the best diet for your dogs, cats or other domesticated animals, but it's the only way to avoid lost time and greater expense. It appears that finding a veterinarian that prescribes raw diets, specific to the pet's body type and needs, which generalized diets do not factor, would be the safest solution.

Alternatively doing your research and discovering different methods is a possibility. Providing a raw and fresh cut of meat every day can be difficult and expensive, and you can find minimally cooked recipes that allow you to prepare several meals at a time and refrigerate but avoid freezing most foods as it damages the nutrients and enzymes.

There are minimally cooked and processed packaged foods available that are healthier than those that contain powdered cellulose (wood pulp) as a filler, which is an insoluble fiber and does not break down in the digestive tract or have any nutritional value. Read your ingredient labels and you will find it in many of our processed foods, such as shredded cheese, bread, ice cream, and various frozen foods.

My son has a small dog that underwent anesthesia to have his teeth cleaned when he was seven years old, which we now know to be very dangerous, especially for small dogs. His weight greatly increased, despite prescribed and extreme decreases in the prescribed food, and he lost his energy and playfulness. He was taken to a second veterinarian, who determined that something had damaged his pancreas, which normally secretes enzymes into the small intestines to break down fats, carbs and proteins, and releases insulin to regulate blood sugar. The veterinarian prescribed medications and a processed food that he hoped would help.

Unfortunately, there was no improvement, and my son called me in distress. I lent an ear while he decided to prepare the dog's meals with raw ingredients that were teeming with enzymes to compensate for the lack thereof, which would wishfully help him to process his food and absorb the nutrients. After much research and consideration, he developed an evolving diet that reversed the condition, and his dog is now seventeen years old.

Animals can overcome most bacteria and impurities in water, but not chlorine, fluoride and other toxins found in most public water systems. They should drink chemical-free water, just as we should.

h2o

There is no unbiased evidence that fluoride pastes have any dental benefits, only experiments where a coating was applied to some surfaces and not others. Of course, any type of coating will delay decay in comparison to a bare surface, but we cannot walk around with coated teeth and there are no benefits to drinking fluoride. The Grand Rapids study was used to get approval for widespread water fluoridation, and they had to claim that it was not harmful because it had already been released onto an entire city.

Fluoride is a naturally occurring poison administered in low doses to mask the effect, and overexposure or consumption gradually causes long-term health issues, so why is it in our toothpastes and water systems?

Complacency is defined as *self-satisfaction, especially when accompanied by unawareness of actual dangers or deficiencies*. Adolf Hitler's scientists discovered that fluoride would make the population complacent and easier to manipulate, and the Nazis were the first to implement water fluoridation. Fluoride also calcifies the pineal gland and separates us from spirituality, which is at the top of the elite's agenda.

For some reason, perhaps because they have seen someone do this on television, or see it as a freeing ceremonial practice, some flush unwanted medications down the toilet and into water systems. Many molecules found in medications, cleaning solutions and runoff from lawn chemicals are as small as one micron. They easily flow through the coarse filters used to recirculate the wastewater and many are impervious to the chemical sanitation process. Let's not even get me started on intentional pollution.

Fortunately, "dirty" water is one of the easier problems to solve. *Osmosis* is *a process by which the molecules of a solvent equalize with a solution through a semi-permeable membrane*. All that's required to reverse the process is pressure. Salt and impurities down to one half micron in size are separated from water as it forced through a thin layer of Gore Tex in the method known as reverse osmosis. Electrolytes and other minerals are also removed but can be added after filtration, and there are other methods of sufficient filtration and options for higher alkaline levels. Most water filters, such as pitcher and refrigerator filters, provide between five and fifteen-microns filtration and only reduce odor and improve taste. The fluoride, chlorine and other toxic molecules remain and shade the cells over time.

I shudder to think about the amount of toxins I ingested before realizing these things; all the bottled water packaged in BPA, *Bisphenol A, an industrial chemical used for manufacturing plastics and epoxy resins* and a byproduct of petroleum. Heat, and especially sunlight, cause BPA and other plastic molecules to seep into the water or beverage. Now I notice cases of products sitting in the sun outside convenience stores after being heated in trucks during the shipping process and feel sorry for those that drink them. We should also avoid hot food served in plastic containers, as well as Styrofoam, which leaches styrene into the contained foods and beverages.

Typical Topical Solutions

It would be wise to consider the adverse effects of toxic topical products, which are often listed as "dermatologist approved" and "doctor recommended" but affect millions of unsuspecting consumers.

Parabens, preservatives found in over thirteen thousand beauty products, are estrogenic, and inhibit hormonal balance by blocking estrogen receptors. Some manufacturers switched to phenoxyethanol after parabens were proven harmful, but studies show that it causes skin irritation, reproductive and developmental complications, and brain and nervous system damage. A natural preservative solution to look for is sodium benzoate, and products will have a shorter shelf life as it is not a synthetic chemical.

Phthalates, found in many body lotions, deodorants, nail polishes, and scented lip balms, are often not listed on product labels because fragrances are classified as proprietary information. It seems the only way to avoid them is to not use any products with "fragrances" listed in the ingredients. The University of Maryland performed a study and concluded that males exposed to phthalates have higher rates of infertility and reproductive issues, and lower testosterone levels. Females have a higher rate of premature deliveries and are prone to endometriosis (uterus cell tissue outside the uterine cavity).

Benzoyl peroxide, commonly used in acne medications, irritates the eyes and respiratory system, and is directly linked to the growth of tumors. Our skin needs the good bacteria it kills to function normally. Triclosan, found in most hand sanitizers, kills necessary bacteria and affects thyroid hormones.

Resorcinol, a chemical commonly found in hair dyes, affects the nervous system, adrenal gland and thyroid function. The symptoms include nausea, abdominal pain, unconsciousness, and skin irritation.

Hydroquinone, the most common ingredient in skin products that aid with acne scars, age spots and sun damage, is carcinogenic (having the potential to cause cancer) and reduces skin elasticity. Mineral oil and petrolatum are petroleum byproducts, which contain carcinogens absorbed in production.

Methylisothiazolinone, a biocide (kills microorganisms) found in many shampoos, conditioners, hair colors, laundry and dish detergents, body washes, and hand soaps, is a proven cause of brain damage.

In the year 2008, the Center for Disease Control and Prevention reported that most Americans were contaminated with oxybenzone, a chemical used in many sunscreens to absorb UVA and UVB rays. It mimics hormones, causes infertility, and creates an imbalance that promotes ideal conditions for cancer.

There are naturally occurring alternatives that allow us to avoid most of those toxins, such as zinc oxide-based sunscreens. We should also try to avoid products that contain heavy metals, such as aluminum in deodorants.

The Smoking Gun

You might notice the pattern that is developing here. A multitude of sources are most often the cause behind cell toxicity and poor health. We tend to look for a single solution when symptoms recur, and often overlook the fact that numerous choices, habits and circumstances over time are the true culprits.

Most medications only treat symptoms and inhibit proper diagnosis of the underlying causes of the condition, and there can be one or several sources- not necessarily one thing to discover. Let's suppose someone starts having frequent headaches or stomachaches and takes an over-the-counter drug to get relief. It works and they take it as the condition returns, until a prescription drug is needed to get relief. Eventually tests and scans are performed in an attempt to determine and isolate a single source as the condition becomes unbearable, all while remaining unaware of the factors that initiated the process.

Headache and pain medications, excluding some anti-inflammatory products, only target neural pathways and block pain receptors. They do nothing to improve the condition, which always gets worse because we cannot feel the continuing damage. Acetaminophen, the widely used over-the-counter ingredient, does not break down in the body and causes liver and kidney damage. Dizziness, vertigo and cognitive issues can be experienced as collective amounts flow through the brain. Tramadol, a popular prescription pain reliever, is an opioid, causing liver, kidney, heart, and cognitive issues.

Sometimes there is a smoking gun, and sometimes it is overlooked, especially when diagnosing mental health conditions. Psychiatrists were the only doctors that did not view the part of the body they were treating. Thanks to Dr. Daniel Amen and others embracing the practice of performing brain scans for abnormalities before blindly prescribing medications, conditions can be promptly and accurately diagnosed without the typical trial and error and often treated with enhancement activities or surgery. That is a step in the right direction, but the most overlooked factor in poor mental health is diet. We cannot expect brain cells that are undernourished and overwhelmed by chemicals to function properly.

If you do not wish to make any improvements to your diet, it might be best to skip these related sections. If I convince you that most of the available foods and beverages are harmful, and you continue to consume them, the negative effects will be multiplied by your knowledge and belief.

Excitotoxins

I once saw an eighty-five-year-old man being interviewed after he had just completed a triathlon. He attributed his longevity and level of fitness to not putting anything in his body without knowing all the ingredients and effects. Let's make the association between "dirty" food and poor health and bring to your attention the necessity of becoming aware of the toxins most people unwittingly consume, by not taking the time to read labels and investigate the ingredients they put in their bodies. Eventually you will have very few labels to read because you will be consuming much less processed food.

You will find that over ninety percent of the products available at your local grocery store are more toxic than nutritious, and that is how we should determine what to consume; toxins versus nutrients. Walking the aisles of the supermarkets, we find colorful packaging and enticing statements designed to overshadow the contents. Red and orange appeal to your desires, yellow influences your will and blue gains your trust. You might notice that all fast-food restaurants use those colors for the same purpose.

The shocking truth is almost all processed foods contain *excitotoxins*, a term used by Dr. Edward Group, DC to classify *highly addictive chemical compounds capable of overstimulating and damaging brain neurons*. There are hundreds of these chemicals, and many are used as cigarette additives, making them and some commercial foods more addictive than cocaine. Here are just a few of the most common and dangerous examples:

Monosodium Glutamate (MSG) is naturally produced in the body to induce cell termination, and dietary glutamate is a powerful enhancer that crosses the blood-brain barrier and triggers brain cell death, with the initial side effect as headaches. Many people with recurring migraines would be cured if they simply stopped consuming MSG, which is not easy because it is well-hidden in the ingredients. It's often listed as "natural flavors, flavoring, hydrolyzed vegetable protein, autolyzed protein, textured protein, plant protein, yeast extract, nutritional yeast, carrageenan", and other types of glutamate.

Aspartic Acid, or aspartate, is a non-essential amino acid that triggers NMDA receptors and initiates cell death, resulting in headaches, seizures and sleep disorders. Commonly known as aspartame; it is a confirmed carcinogen found in almost all diet foods and drinks, breakfast cereals, cake mixes, sweeteners, gums, mints, candies, and cough drops.

Cysteine is created by hydrolysis of human hair and poultry feathers and reacts with sugar to achieve savory meat flavors in the Maillard reaction. It is known to be a direct cause of Parkinson's and Alzheimer's diseases.

You could begin to stop buying and consuming toxic foods the easy way or the hard way. I chose the difficult route and began reading labels on the items in my cabinet. Almost everything I had was placed in a couple of storage containers and labeled "emergency only", until it expired and was discarded.

The process of reading labels in the store was difficult and time consuming, and I rarely found a food that passed the test. I eventually defaulted to the easy way and stopped buying processed foods, with the exception of organic, minimally processed, additive-free nut butters, pastas, sauces, and grains.

GMO

Growing the same crop over and over again in the same location depletes the soil and destroys the plant's immunity to insects and fungi. Pesticides and fungicides are applied, which further weakens the crop and introduces toxins. Immunity is achieved by the bugs and fungi, but stronger chemicals would certainly kill the crop, unless you modify the genetic structure to have immunity from those chemicals.

Genetically Modified Organisms (GMO) were implemented as a solution, instead of alternating crops and replenishing the soil. The use of petroleum-based fertilizers, with only nitrogen, phosphorous and potassium nutrients, inhibits immunity and increases toxicity, and the entire process renders almost all commercial food products unfit for consumption. Current GMO crops include soy, corn, canola, sugar beets, potatoes, alfalfa, papaya, and summer squash, and commercial wheat and apples have a pesticide added to their composition. All should be avoided, and most can be replaced with organic counterparts.

Organic corn is a healthy superfood, and some potatoes, whole wheat, apples, and the other crops are often fine when organically grown; however, soy is harmful, regardless of how it is grown. If you have met a vegetarian that looked unhealthy, soy is likely the reason. Many consume it for protein when they stop eating meat, which is jumping out of the frying pan and into the fire. I have also seen it prescribed for lactose intolerance, which provides some initial relief, until the soy accumulates in the system and a hormonal imbalance is created by the isoflavones, which mimic estrogen in the body, while goitrogens block iodine absorption and inhibit proper thyroid function. Some of the eventual side effects include bloating, cramps, constipation, diarrhea, hives, itching, difficulty in breathing, and high blood pressure.

A form of GMO soy, canola or corn, such as corn syrup and high fructose corn syrup, can be found in almost every processed food. Please look at your mayo, ketchup, sauces, and salad dressing labels and you will find at least one in all non-organic products, and most organic salad dressings contain soy. An otherwise healthy salad is rendered toxic, unless you make your own dressing or find a soy-free option. Most restaurants fry with soybean seed oil, and some use corn or canola seed oil, all GMO, which are absorbed into the fried food and responsible for a laundry list of compounded issues over time.

Organic simply means something is derived from living matter, and is free from chemical fertilizers, pesticides and other artificial agents. Growing your own food or finding a cooperative grow situation is obviously the best solution, and something we should all plan and learn for several reasons. Until then, naturally grown food from small or verifiably organic farms is the best way to avoid toxins. Some small farms grow naturally but are not certified and large corporations often take advantage of poor regulation.

Lactose Intolerant

The human body is not designed or intended to consume lactic acid in any form. Lactose intolerance is diagnosed for those that have immediate or stronger reactions, which leads many to believe that it's okay for the rest of us. Lactic acid forms in the muscles and milk of all animals, and no other species drinks the milk of another for good reason. A cow's milk is naturally and specifically formulated for calves, which we are not. It is toxic to all human beings and should not be consumed, especially in the processed form. The heating during pasteurization kills any beneficial components, and the synthetic vitamins listed are added after the process, which is also true for pasteurized orange juice and other fruit juices that are basically sugar water.

Baby cows need lots of sustenance, and dairy products are highly concentrated forms of lactic acid. The average cheese is roughly eighty percent fat, and low-fat cheese is rarely lower than seventy, which makes it almost impossible for anyone that consumes cheese and other dairy products to lose weight. A typical mistake many make when dieting is eating less of the same foods, instead of eliminating the unhealthy and calorie-rich ones.

Parmesan and Romano are two hard cheeses with dietary benefits that can be enjoyed in moderation if they are in whole form, and you grate it yourself to avoid cellulose powder. Zero-sugar Greek yogurt can be beneficial as a source of protein and critical live probiotic bacteria for good gut health.

The China Study, by T. Colin Campbell, PhD and Thomas M. Campbell, MD, documents over two decades of research in partnership with Cornell, Oxford and the Chinese Academy of Preventative Medicine. They tied the consumption of animal protein-based foods to the development of cancer and heart disease, stating that casein (a protein in milk) is "the most relevant carcinogen ever identified".

Further studies by T. Colin Campbell bring good news to any that cannot imagine life without eating meat. Lowering the consumed amount to less than twenty percent of your total caloric intake allows the body to "buffer" the lactic acid and overcome most of the adverse effects. That is by calories- not how much room it takes up on the plate. It will be a drastic reduction for people that consume meat or dairy three meals per day. The benefits would extend far beyond personal health by greatly reducing the amount of required feed, methane gas and cruelty associated with the process of animal farming.

Dr. Caldwell B. Esselstyn Jr., MD leads the cardiovascular prevention and reversal program at the Cleveland Clinic Wellness Institute. After more than two decades of global research, they discovered that cardiovascular disease and cancer were extremely rare in people who ate plant-based diets. "To do one study, we recruited twenty-four patients from the clinic's cardiovascular department, people who had basically been told to go home and prepare for death, and put them on a plant-based diet. Every one of them who followed the diet lived without any more incidents of heart disease. Cardiovascular disease is a toothless paper tiger that need never exist. And if it does exist, it need never progress. It is a food-borne illness. Change your food, and you change your life." The man made his living performing heart and breast cancer surgeries and decided to decrease the amount of patients rather than see them continue to arrive in growing numbers, and he will only treat those that agree to stop consuming animal protein.

An implanted concern many have with plant-based diets is lack of protein, but most are likely getting more than they need. Various vegetables are very high in protein, and most contain moderate amounts. Nuts and seeds can be good sources, and hemp seeds contain all essential amino acids. Beans, brown rice, pastas, whole grains, and quinoa, which contains all essential amino acids, are also good sources.

World-class athletes that make the switch experience increased strength, speed and endurance. My favorite example is when Carl Lewis outperformed his younger self in his third Olympic Games and was very competitive in his fourth. Plant-based diets will improve anyone's performance and health, as well as decrease odor and perspiration. You will only perspire when you are hot or strenuously exercising after the lactic acid level is sufficiently reduced.

Dr. Terry Mason, MD refers to erectile dysfunction as "the canary in the coal mine". It is a result of poor circulation and often the first symptom of cardiovascular disease. There is an increasing number of cases in younger men, which could easily be corrected by not eating anything that once had parents. The only foods our bodies are designed to consume are grown in the ground- not born and raised.

Staples

Rather than describing issues with every food and beverage, we will take a look at some of the typical choices that comprise the average American diet: Pizza is highly addictive due to the amount of processed sugar in the crust. A slice has as much as two large cookies, and the flour is not whole wheat, it's "enriched" with excitotoxins and a genetic pesticide. The sauce is from cans lined with BPA, and the processed meat and cheese are high in lactic acid, growth hormones, antibiotics, preservatives, and fat. Making your own pizza, with fresh organic ingredients, is a way to satisfy your taste buds and avoid the toxins. There are jarred organic sauces and prepared organic crusts of various types for less labor, just remember to watch out for added sugar.

A peanut butter and jelly sandwich seems harmless, and some might even consider it nutritious. The average bread contains enriched wheat, sugar or high fructose corn syrup, and MSG is often a hidden ingredient. The jelly most likely contains high fructose corn syrup, artificial coloring, and hidden excitotoxins listed as "natural flavors". The peanut butter is high in calories, saturated fat, processed sugar, and sodium. It can contain aflatoxin, a form of carcinogenic mold, which is more common in unprocessed peanuts. Organic whole-wheat bread, preserves and almond butter would be a better choice.

Macaroni and cheese mixes contain toxic wheat, whey (a byproduct of cheese production), milk protein concentrate, milkfat, sodium, added lactic acid, and hidden phthalates are a common additive.

Sushi is a quick and easy grab at the supermarket, and it was a reasonably healthy food for Asian cultures in the distant past. Increased mercury levels in water have resulted in high levels in fish and shellfish. Being more selective helps, as some types are naturally less contaminated. Skipjack tuna, also used in canned light tuna, contains three times less mercury than the larger albacore and ahi (yellowfin and bigeye), as it has a higher level of selenium, which is an essential mineral for antioxidant defense.

Tilapia is a food we should avoid. It is cheaper than most fish due to the inexpensive and undesirable raising, but the main issue is the low amount of omega-3 fatty acids, which are anti-inflammatory, and the high amount of omega-6 fatty acids, which are inflammatory. Wild-caught salmon is a much healthier option, and it has many beneficial properties; however, fish are animals that contain lactic acid and mercury, and moderation is wise.

The prevalent iceberg lettuce is mostly water, so it's great for hydration but has almost no nutritional value. Dark, leafy greens, such as kale, spinach, arugula, collard greens, mustard greens, bok choy, and chard, are high in fiber, vitamins, iron, calcium, magnesium, and other vital nutrients.

Dishonorable mention for processed foods goes to all the genetically modified, sugar-infested breakfast cereals that are found in many cupboards.

I ran into an old friend at the store who was on his way to see a doctor that had diagnosed him as having IBS (irritable bowel syndrome), beginning late morning and remaining throughout the day. It was his fourth appointment, and he was on his second prescription medication, which was not helping the condition. I asked what he was drinking in the mornings, and it was coffee. I suggested he try an organic coffee, and he called with thanks a few weeks later because his condition had greatly improved. Coffee is a resilient crop that can withstand high amounts of pesticides and fungicides, which it retains and delivers to the consumer's system, and mycotoxins (a mold byproduct) are common due to poor regulation. Verifiably organic coffee is considered healthy when moderately consumed, as it is high in beneficial potassium.

Sports, energy, protein, and soft drinks, bottled and boxed juices, and other processed beverages are often alarmingly high in added sugar and can contain microplastics and other toxins. Unsweetened green tea with honey and fresh-squeezed lemon juice is my favorite beverage, while organic fruits satisfy my cravings for sweets, and I get a natural sugar "fix".

You will find many healthy and satisfying alternatives if you decide to pursue change. Please do not let my choices discourage or influence you. I am only relaying a few of the alternatives that work well for some of us. Even if I was an experienced nutritionist, which I'm not, it is unsafe to advise anyone what to eat and not eat, without knowing their individual needs through bloodwork and examination. Be cautious of advice from anyone that does not have that knowledge and leery of all generalized diets.

One of the phrases I was referring to earlier that lost its value over time is, "You are what you eat", which was derived from Jean Anthelme Brillat-Savarin's book published in the year 1825 and titled The Physiology of Taste, in which he wrote, "Tell me what you eat, and I will tell you what you are". His intent was to convey the fact that our diets heavily influence our health, well-being and personality.

Supplements have become a staple for those who eat deficient foods and attempt to get nutrients from concentrated pills or powders. It is a form of pharmacology, and most of the brands are owned by mega corporations like Proctor & Gamble, Nestle and Pfizer. Some also own fast food chains and get lots of business from the same customers. Most people buy the cheapest brands they can find, which are likely contaminated with petroleum, heavy metals and pesticides. There is a lack of regulation, and the labels can inaccurately reflect the actual ingredients, as well as the amount of each ingredient, resulting in excessive or inadequate doses. Medication and food interactions can be very dangerous, and products marketed for bodybuilding and weight loss often contain undeclared steroids and similar substances.

It is always best to get nutrients from our food, but there are deficiencies and circumstances where supplements are necessary. Simply taking a multivitamin to supplement any deficiencies is a shot in the dark, which also results in excessive or inadequate doses. People over fifty can have high levels of iron in their blood, as the body does not have an efficient way to expel it, which causes damage to the liver, heart and pancreas. Others can have iron deficiency anemia and require a supplement and a way to help the body absorb it, such as vitamin C. All supplements should be specific to your needs and organically produced, and you can research reputable brands and check for third-party testing and certification to help avoid poor regulation.

Timing is an important factor and a potential issue. High doses of supplements can saturate the cells and prevent absorption of other nutrients when taken with meals, while some must be taken with food.

Don't Bring It Home

Meals eaten at restaurants or as a guest in someone's home became a big issue after changing my diet. Restaurants cannot compete by serving organic food, and those that do are often too expensive for my budget. I was excited about the changes and once made the mistake of explaining why I no longer ate certain foods when refusing them, unleashing the placebo effect on those who were about to eat them. It was rude and inconsiderate, and there is a time and place to discuss such things. We tend to go to extremes when making changes, until the excitement and passion decline enough to achieve balance.

I came to believe that offending the host was more harmful to my body than eating what was served, and now I bless those meals and enjoy them, occasionally stating that I prefer not to eat some foods, but without further explanation. I do my best at restaurants and try not to worry about the adverse effects, which only makes them worse. A couple ways to avoid over-indulgence are to rarely eat out and never bring toxic food or drink home.

Excluding meat from my grocery list allows me to afford organic fruits, vegetables, grains, and other healthy foods, and that is all I can find in my kitchen when I get a meat or junk food craving. It makes it easier to keep lactic acid and toxins under harmful levels when they are less accessible.

There are natural remedies for almost every condition. We just have to look for them and ensure they will not cause any negative reactions when combined with other foods or drugs. Turmeric is a natural pain reliever and a powerful anti-inflammatory, which also aids in digestion, improves liver and brain function, prevents acne, treats psoriasis, and increases immunity.

It is not easily absorbed by the cells, unless it is dissolved in almond or coconut milk, or some other source of healthy fat, and black pepper will help with that process. There are many medications that should not be taken with turmeric, such as diabetes, liver and anti-inflammatory drugs, blood thinners, pain relievers, antihistamines, and antacids.

It should not be consumed at the same time with spinach in large portions, garlic, ginger, fatty fish, coffee, alcohol, dairy products, iron supplements, sugar, or sodium. That did not take long to research, and the curcumin in turmeric is one of the more interactive substances. Most natural solutions that you research will be less complicated, but we must become aware of the potential issues when introducing new remedies, and consider the interactions between our current foods, supplements and drugs.

I recently discovered that consuming carrots with cucumbers nullifies the numerous benefits of the cucumber, unless combined with fresh lemon juice or vinegar. Bananas must be avoided, and excessive sodium is harmful when eaten with cucumber, which makes pickles unhealthy if they contain too much salt. Pears pair well with them, and apples and vinegar enhance the nutritional value of this superfood.

I mentioned that yogurt can be beneficial, but not when consumed with citrus fruits and melons, which induce fermentation, increase acidity and inhibit digestion. High-protein and spicy foods should also be avoided. Beneficial inclusions are chia and flax seeds, oats, apples, and bananas.

Heavy metal accumulation in the body is an escalating issue. Our air, water, soil, and food are heavily contaminated with aluminum, barium, cadmium, lead, arsenic, mercury, and more. The body's ability to expel such things is greatly enhanced by lowering the toxin intake and consuming the right foods. This is another benefit of turmeric, and cilantro, garlic, cruciferous vegetables, such as broccoli, cauliflower, kale, arugula, radish, cabbage, brussels sprouts, and small portions of broccoli sprouts are great allies.

Microplastics are a legitimate and growing concern. Less than ten percent of plastics are recycled. It is an expensive process, and it's much more economical to use fossil fuel waste. We are deceived into separately disposing of plastics to support the false belief that we are not harming the environment, to the extent that the recycled symbols on most new plastics closely resemble the actual symbol but are often faked.

Plastic never goes away; it can only change forms. Some of the waste is incinerated into toxic gas and the rest winds up in our oceans, contaminating marine life and becoming inseparable from salt, which is why we should only consume Himalayan pink or ancient sea salts, without modern contamination.

Up to thirty percent more microplastics collect in brain tissue than the liver and kidneys, and they are not easily expelled. The average person now has seven grams of plastic in their brain. Reducing the use of plastics and consuming the right foods is the best and only defense in environmental protection and detoxification. We can choose products in glass jars whenever possible, store food in glass containers and use stainless steel water bottles, cleaning them regularly. We should avoid plastic utensils, cutting boards, toothbrushes, dental floss, scrub brushes, baby bottles, coffee filters, coffee pods, dishwasher pods, metal food and beverage cans, which are lined with plastic, and throw out any Teflon cookware.

There are non-toxic alternatives, such as metal utensils, titanium and marble cutting boards, bamboo toothbrushes, plastic-free floss, biodegradable coffee filters, and glass baby bottles fitted with silicone nipples. Some foods that help us to expel microplastics are garlic, onions, milk thistle, and cruciferous vegetables. A bare minimum of seven hours of uninterrupted deep sleep in total or near-total darkness and frequent intermittent or periodic long fasting are critical to enhance *autophagy*, which is *the process of cells degrading and recycling damaged or dysfunctional components, effectively cleaning and renewing themselves*. Improving autophagy, upgrading diet, changing habits, and meditating will allow you to become and remain holistically healthy, but will require getting out of your comfort zone.

Fasting can be uncomfortable for beginners, but if you can get through the initial hunger, the healing process will begin. It takes fourteen hours for the cells to fully recover from digesting meals and divert their energy to other functions, and a minimum of sixteen hours is needed to stimulate autophagy on a regular basis. That can easily be accomplished by finishing dinner by six o'clock and eating breakfast or brunch after ten o'clock; although, eighteen or more hours between meals is better for intermittent fasting.

Long fasting weekly, biweekly or monthly for twenty-four to thirty-six hours will induce many more benefits. At fourteen hours insulin levels decline, and the body begins using stored fat for fuel. Around twenty-four hours men get a two thousand percent increase in human growth hormone production and women get a thirteen hundred percent increase, which preserves muscle, burns fat, protects brain cells, repairs skin cells, and slows the aging process. Gut stem cell activation also occurs at this time, healing and regenerating the area where seventy percent of the body's immune system resides and fortifying the first line of defense against toxins, infections and inflammation. At thirty-six hours all benefits enhance, and the mind enters a heightened state as it seems that we must be searching for food.

Green tea is beneficial when fasting as it contains epigallocatechin gallate (EGCG), a polyphenol with antioxidant and anti-inflammatory properties. Research is required for a healthy meal to break the fast, which is determined by your individual needs and goals. High-fiber and low-sugar foods are best.

Dental health is a very important part of overall health that we should probably examine and rethink. Alternatives to having the protective enamel scraped off every six months become available to those that stop consuming processed sugar, and root canals can create more issues than they temporarily solve. Many people fail to make the association between the hidden infection and recurring conditions. Depending on the situation, it's probably best to get the dead tooth out and explore other options.

To Heat Or Not To Heat

We live in a society that glorifies egotistical, condescending television chefs, who promote the practices and ingredients that result in poor health. The process of heating food destroys the enzymes and damages the nutrients; fortunately, studies show that if fifty percent of our caloric intake is raw and unprocessed, the body will use those enzymes to help accept, process and absorb the cooked portion of the meal. A side salad with a steak and baked potato would not achieve that ratio. You can make your salad and vegetable or fruit medley to include a variety of organic superfoods, and some of the side dishes you normally cook could be served raw or lightly heated to help reach the essential amount of "alive" food.

We can try not to overcook that which must be cooked, such as pasta, rice, beans, and potatoes, and keep in mind that some foods, such as tomatoes, are more beneficial when moderately heated as the process increases absorption.

I was in my teens when microwave ovens were introduced. There was a lot of concern about safety from radiation outside the cavity but very few were concerned with putting things inside the cavity. I came to believe that microwaving food is one of the biggest contributors to our current epidemic of poor health. Traditional methods of heating food eventually rearrange and damage the molecules. Microwave ovens rearrange the food molecules to generate the heat, which instantly destroys all the enzymes and nutrients.

That thin metal mesh in the door prevents the low-frequency waves from leaving the cavity, and they would not travel very far anyway. The technology has been weaponized for crowd control by using high-frequency waves. The long waves in the oven cavity deeply penetrate, which is why the food cooks from the inside out. The short waves projected at people do not over-penetrate; they travel farther and severely burn the epidermis. Some protesters are putting aluminum foil on the backs of their signs to block the radiation, and as crazy as it sounds, aluminum foil hats and metal mesh gloves are beneficial if you choose to outwardly battle a condition.

Our digestive capabilities decline as we age, and some people can experience difficulty in processing some raw foods. Briefly heating at a low temperature aids in digestion with minimal damage. Adequate cleaning of raw fruits and vegetables is necessary to rid harmful bacteria. You can soak them in a bowl with a solution ratio of one part vinegar to four parts water for ten to fifteen minutes and thoroughly rinse.

Union

No single habit improved my quality of life more than Yoga; although, meditation and proper diet have also been invaluable. You can regain most of the flexibility and vibrant energy you possessed as a child with time, patience and perseverance. Yoga also improves immunity, blood pressure, circulation, respiration, arthritis, injury resistance, sleep, anxiety, stress, depression, balance, and coordination. You will find that you can stretch a little farther and feel a little better each session if you stick with it.

The key is frequency, in more ways than one. Taking a weekly class to initiate is recommended but you might not realize any significant results, unless you practice frequently and hold some positions longer than the group might. Practicing once a week and holding positions for thirty seconds will only maintain previous gains. We must engage twice a week and hold most positions for one minute or longer to make continual progress, and three or four sessions per week to maximize. Of course, make sure there are no issues that would make Yoga unsafe for you, and never overdo any good practice, allowing the body sufficient time to recover. *Yoga* is a Sanskrit word meaning union, which intends *to unite with the Divine*. Mindful breathing is part of the process, and the combination raises your vibrational frequency.

Tai Chi, or Taijiquan (supreme boundary movement), is an extremely beneficial ancient Chinese practice that combines motion with meditation. Created as a form of self-defense, it is a method to cultivate a form of power that has no boundary and can be less strenuous and difficult than Yoga.

Everyone agrees that exercise is a critical part of health, longevity and energy levels, and there is no shortage of available information, so we will just touch a few bases and address a few misconceptions:

Cardiovascular and resistance training are equally important; they just have different benefits. Cardio provides more immediate energy and burns more calories, while resistance increases muscle mass and longevity. High intensity interval training (HIIT) has been proven to be the best method for both forms.

A runner, swimmer or cyclist might go hard for thirty to sixty seconds and slow down for sixty to ninety seconds, allowing the heart to speed up and recover over a continuing cycle. Intense exercise over long periods maintains a consistently fast heart rate, which our bodies are not designed to do, and there are numerous cases of athletes with resulting complications after marathons and similar events.

For the average person, the amount of weight lifted and number of sets and repetitions performed in most resistance training are less important than ensuring the muscles are eventually worked to failure with moderate weights, bands, push-ups. pull-ups, sit-ups, squats, lunges, and all other body-weight exercises. Bodybuilding should be more scientific and precise, with varying weight, sets and repetitions, depending on the goal, strength, mass or tone.

Warming up and cooling down are very important in all forms of exercise, and we should never work or stretch cold muscles. A quick walk or brief calisthenics before stretching prior to exercise is best and gradually bring the heart rate back to normal during cool down, then stretch again. Stretching prior to exercise is different from Yoga. Holding the positions too long and far will weaken the muscles, reduce performance and possibly lead to injury. Thirty to forty seconds for each muscle group before and after exercise is ideal and should be performed within ten minutes of the start and completion.

Working a specific part of the body does not burn fat in that specific area. Stored fat will be removed as it was applied and only used when there is no other source of energy. Performing sit-ups or crunches builds and tones the targeted muscles but does not burn fat from the stomach area, and a common mistake is not developing the back. The stronger muscles overpower the opposing ones and create an imbalance that leads to discomfort and injury. The quadriceps and hamstring opposition is another area to balance.

The lymphatic system is described as the body's vacuum cleaner but is not stimulated by muscular contraction in the same way as veins and arteries. Safely bouncing up and down on a rebounder (fitness tramp) or performing jumping jacks for one minute in the mornings will help move the waste to the lymph nodes to be filtered. The calf muscles act as the body's second heart, pumping used blood back up to the heart, and the jumping aids in that process. Calf raises and other leg exercises are also beneficial.

We all remember being told to wait an hour after meals before swimming to avoid cramps, which is fine and well, but more time is required before engaging in strenuous exercise. Three to four hours is much better, especially when performing yoga and applying pressure along the digestive tract. The morning is the best time to exercise, before meals, distractions and daily restrictions. It is also the best opportunity to burn stored fat for fuel, and the cells become charged and ready to absorb the next meal.

Fare Well

I wish you to be charged and ready to accept the process of life and the abundance of the Universe, and that often means achieving stability and focus, so I will leave you with a few techniques:

A simple way to help control emotions is to separate yourself from them, by ridding mentalities, such as I *am* angry or I *am* sad, and realizing that we only *feel* angry or sad, and it's just a state of mind that we can change.

In order to calm, center and be in the moment, you can ask yourself and observe; what do I see, what do I hear and what do I feel?

You might try the box breathing exercise if you need to nip stress at the bud: Inhale, hold in, exhale, and hold out your breath, performing each stage to a consistent count of four.

Another form of meditation for beginners is to sit quietly and allow your thought to wander for a few minutes prior to entering the meditative state. It might even consume the entire session, but still effectively quiets the mind, and much is prioritized or resolved during that time.

It seems unnecessary to summarize this collection of thoughts, and the subtitles should make it easy to review anything that interest you before doing your own research. Much remains between the lines of the condensed descriptions of the Essene and other philosophies for you to discover at your leisure. Have you ever researched a car that interested you and began to notice that model everywhere? Pure intentions reveal an abundance of what we seek, so trust your instincts, stay the course, and you will walk the path.

Namaste

I honor the place in you in which the entire Universe dwells
I honor the place in you that is of love, of truth, of light, and of peace
When you are in that place in you, and I am in that place in me
We are One

Credits & References

"What has been will be again, what has been done will be done again; there is nothing new under the Sun" - Ecclesiastes 1:9. A modern interpretation is that originality is an illusion, history repeats itself and we cannot change anything. I partially disagree. Cycles exist to be improved upon or broken.

A simpler meaning is that all information and ideas are currently existing, which also serves as my disclaimer. Some of the realizations I described occurred when I began to educate myself without a curriculum and were only affirmed after I began to explore them. It is not my intent to copy anyone.

I give credit and thanks to the living souls that introduced me to existing information or expanded my knowledge, while maintaining that my writings do not necessarily reflect their descriptions or intent. Of course, the quotes are credited, and I am grateful to those mentioned with their information.

I heard the story of the Native American's first encounter with ships while enjoying one of Dolores Cannon's speeches. I cannot know if it is true, but it certainly opened my mind to become more aware. Noam Chomsky was the main source for the media, propaganda and manufacture of consent, and the descriptions of serpent worship, paganism, secret societies, ancient practices, and the elite's agenda were heavily influenced by several books and documentaries from Phillip Gardner and Ben Stewart.

The Strawman Illusion is well-explained in Mary Elizabeth Croft's book, How I Clobbered Every Bureaucratic Cash-confiscatory Agency Known To Man and The Errant Sovereign's Handbook, Volumes I and II by Augustus Blackstone. Please keep in mind that sovereignty is more of a state of mind than a statement, and the ability to maintain the distinction between you and your strawman is more important than attempting to undo the many ties that bind you to the system and its jurisdiction.

Amit Goswami was the first scientist that awakened me to connect the physical significance and spiritual relevance of quantum mechanics, so I went to a used bookstore and found The Universe In A Single Atom, The Convergence Of Science And Spirituality by the 14th Dalai Lama, Lhamo Thondup. It is the perfect book for any that wish to initiate themselves.

Many of the deeper truths, scientific experiments and spiritual discoveries were sourced from Gregg Braden's books, Deep Truth and The Divine Matrix, and my next read is his latest book, Pure Human: The Hidden Truth Of Our Divinity, Power And Destiny, in which he addresses the transhuman movement. My copy of Joseph Weed's book, Wisdom Of The Mystic Masters, has more dog ears and highlights than any other, and I found it to be an incredible single source of spiritual information and practices. A colorful tutorial of the human chakra system, including guided developmental exercises, can be found at Rick Richards's website.

My spiritual understandings and resulting inclusions were formed through decades of consideration, various stages of disbelief, belief and awareness, supporting discoveries by modern science, and the eventual comprehension of the deeper meanings realized in the religious texts sampled and referenced.

Other sources of information and inspiration include Manly P. Hall, Carl Jung, Edgar Cayce, Penney Peirce, Allison Bonds Shapiro, Walter Bradford Cannon, Susan Cain, Richard Gordon, Jason Shurka, John Harris, Owen Waters, Eric Berg, Barbara O'Neill, George Leonard, and Joy Gardner.

I also referenced Webster's, Oxford English and Black's Law Dictionaries, as well as Wikipedia and Google, where I found some of the definitions and summaries to be questionable, misleading or inaccurate. It's becoming more difficult to find anything that undermines the corporate agenda, and many of the sites I sourced, such as The People United Commonwealth (TPUC), were replaced with impostors or taken down to hide the truth and control dissent.

Lettuce Wake cover artwork by R. Burton.

Bless, love and thank you,

Van

Published by Win3Media

ISBN 979-8-9896831-3-0

Copyright 2025 by Van Deburg

Win3Media
Body ~ Mind ~ Spirit

www.ingramcontent.com/pod-product-compliance
Lightning Source LLC
LaVergne TN
LVHW081324110826
845149LV00007B/1590

9798989683130